GOOD
ENOUGH
for
God

" For God so loved..."
John 3:16

Brenda Mason Jones

GOOD ENOUGH
for God

HIS HEART FOR SINNERS
(LIKE ME)

BRENDA MASON YOUNG

Dedication

———

This book is dedicated to the many seekers, strugglers, and sinners who have trusted me with their doubts and questions at Starbucks, in my office, on walks and drives, through emails and Facebook messages, and tearstained handwritten letters. It is my life's joy to see you realize that He delights in you, and you can, indeed, be good enough for God.

Contents

Introduction

Junior high gym class was near the top of my "favorite things to avoid" list. We had it three times weekly, and on far too many occasions, it provided more insecurity than my adolescent psyche needed. Whether it was softball, flag football, volleyball, dodgeball, or any other athletic activity, the teacher's whistle signaled one thing: Line up single file so the captains could begin selecting teams, wildly vying for the best players. I wasn't the worst in the class, but I didn't rank anywhere near the top in anything but volleyball. Even in that sport, my height was a decided disadvantage. I was simply not good enough to be chosen early, and I learned my spot—with roughly eight other girls who were always last to be chosen. It didn't matter that I had several other places where I was recognized for my own abilities. The regular "You're not good enough" message was humiliating, and I dreaded it.

Not unlike my experiences in gym class, the first episodes of each new season of American Idol provide heart-wrenching moments as well. Thousands of young people sacrifice to get an audition, hoping they will be discovered, recognized for a talent that will catapult them into the national spotlight. But only a few get the golden coupon with the "You're going to Hollywood!" inscription. The rest get the devastating evaluation, "You're just not good enough."

No human reaches adulthood without receiving that painful message too many times. Parents mix protective love with their own burning memories to passionately insulate their little ones from evaluation and competition. However, once they enroll in school, the armor melts. By the time we are adults we have been told in a myriad of ways, "You just didn't make the cut. You aren't good enough." Job losses, failed classes, broken relationships, unfaithful partners, unfulfilled dreams—the evidence mounts in a world of constant appraisals that, try as we might, we just aren't enough.

That gives rise to a logical question. If fallible human beings—people who are far from perfect themselves—evaluate us as not good enough, what hope is there of pleasing a holy and perfect God? The Bible says that God is without flaw, infallible, completely just, and with perfect wisdom. The Bible also says that this God wants a relationship with me. With me? How can I possibly be good enough for God?

The route most people take to answer that question has two major signposts: performance and comparison. No one is perfect, but, clearly, some of us are better than others. If I perform better than most or if my good deeds and strong performances outnumber the bad or if I keep improving, then that will make me good enough. Some of us get so good at being good we are totally convinced, if anyone makes the cut, we do. Take me, for instance. Yes, I was and still am lousy at sports, but as an adult in a world devoid of athletic competition, I do pretty well. I've never been arrested, never been addicted or even had any of the habits we commonly define as vices, I've been married faithfully to the same man for decades. Most people think I'm a nice person, I have a ton of friends (Facebook and real), I am kinder than at least 50 percent of the people I know, my kids have become credits to society—that says something about my goodness and parenting, doesn't it? I go to church more than most, and, hey—I even put money in the Salvation Army kettles at Christmas. If I wasn't so infuriatingly humble, I could tell you more. That all counts for something, doesn't it? If we were sorting the world into piles, I am sure I would get in the good pile. Compared to everyone I know, I think I stack up pretty well. I believe I make the cut. I think I am good enough for God.

So who is right? What is right? Is it possible for a sinner like me to be good enough for God? How good do I need to be? The answer is so simple it seems hard to believe. Maybe you have never considered it.

Paul urged the Galatians, "Consider Abraham" (Galatians 3:6 NIV). We're going to do that, because Abraham (originally called Abram, before God changed his name) suffered from all the same doubts and misgivings we do. He got it right sometimes, and sometimes he totally missed the mark. In fact, he made one mistake so significant that it altered the entire course of human history.

In the twenty-first century, we still suffer from the impact of his choice. God's relationship with Abraham leads us to the solid truth, the answer to our question.

The best way to grow from this book:

At the end of each chapter are additional suggestions for thought and action. Don't speed through to the next chapter. Take some time to consider each point, and perhaps even journal your thoughts. Pray that God will lead you in processing His Word so that it will come alive in your daily life.

"Consider Abraham" (Galatians 3:6)

Abram's story begins in the most understated way. It doesn't even sound like a story. It begins, "This is the story of Terah. Terah had Abram, Nahor, and Haran" (Genesis 11:27 MSG). Abram has two brothers, and they both have something he does not: children. That's the first fact we learn about Abram, except for his family members' names—that he is childless.

Abram and his family lived in a degenerate and pagan community. The book of beginnings, Genesis, tells of the creation of the universe and God's loving creation of man and woman. Though the history is condensed and we don't know how swiftly Adam and Eve capitulated to sin, God's original plan and fellowship with mankind in the Garden of Eden ended with just the two first humans. Things got worse with every generation. Their son Cain committed the first murder, and from there the violence and wickedness multiplied. Flagrant depravity was the signpost for the day, and resulted in a planet-wide flood, God's judgment on sin. One man named Noah was a righteous man, still seeking God in the midst of the cultural chaos, and God saved Noah and his family to push the reset button for mankind.

Mankind remained under the spell of Satan, however, and decades and then centuries of deterioration passed after the flood. In a matter of time, the world was X-rated again. That's Genesis 1–11. In the last verses of Genesis 11, we meet Terah and his family, one son named Abram. The whole family lived in a commune of sorts in or near their birthplace of Ur (today northern Iraq, about halfway between the head of the Persian Gulf and the modern city of Baghdad). At that time Ur was one of the most important cities in the world. Because it was adjacent to the Persian Gulf and the Euphrates River, commerce was as easy as could be expected in those days, and it became a trading center.

Archaeological and historical records show that Ur was quite large in its day, covering about four square miles, and that a little more than three hundred thousand residents called it home. Since irrigation gave Ur abundant crops, not everybody needed to work on farms. People learned other skills. Chisel workers sculpted, the gem cutters made jewels, and the fullers used their feet to stomp on woven wools to make them soft and thick. The metal workers crafted weapons. Brick masons made bricks for ziggurats. In the city, the ziggurats stood like modern skyscrapers over the city, some up to seventy feet tall. The culture was educated in mathematics and astronomy, and even preserved their ideas by writing on clay tablets, many of these found by modern archeologists.

The people of Ur worshipped many gods. The one God of Noah had long been forgotten, and the chief deity in this area was the moon god named Nanna. The influence of the culture was strong, and Terah's family was tainted by it, too. Abram grew to become a man and lived for 60 years, surrounded by this wicked and demoralizing society. But God was faithful. He always is.

"The God of glory appeared to our father Abraham while he was still in Mesopotamia, before he lived in Harran. 'Leave your country and your people,' God said, 'and go to the land I will show you'" (Acts 7:2–3 NIV). There is nothing ambivalent or unclear about that command. Despite the fact that God personally appeared and spoke to him, Abram was not completely obedient. He didn't leave his family and friends to follow God; he took them with him. In fact, he allowed his nature-worshipping father Terah to have the driver's seat. Genesis 11 tells us that Terah took his family and possessions and headed for Canaan, the place God had spoken about to his son Abram. (Canaan is the region covering modern Israel, Palestine, Syria, Lebanon, and western parts of Jordan). Abram found it hard to turn his back on family ties and support, particularly because they were leaving the comfortable existence they had known in Ur. So they headed out together.

Perhaps the long, hot journey discouraged them. Maybe the trip was harder than they thought. Perhaps they missed all the conveniences in Ur. Maybe as one day melted into the next they just didn't think it was worth it. Perhaps they were not fully committed to make the move in the first place. For whatever reason, they never reached the goal. They got as far as Haran, a city whose ruins lie within present-day Turkey, a full four hundred miles from their original target. An overnight stay turned into a week and then a month. This was a familiar city. Culturally and religiously, Haran and Ur were sister cities. Soon Canaan was forgotten as they settled into their second choice. Abram lived there with his family until he was seventy-five years old and his father had died.

Not a spectacular resume for a man of his age, regardless of time and culture. He had no children, the currency for significance and fulfillment in his day. The only recorded goal he had attempted in his life, he fell short of reaching. He didn't fully obey God, even after God spoke powerful personal messages to him. Almighty God took the initiative in the beginning to connect with this ordinary man and offer him a partnership. Now He comes to Abram and reaffirms the first words He had spoken:

"Go from your country, your people
and your father's household
to the land I will show you.
I will make you into a great nation,
and I will bless you;
I will make your name great,
and you will be a blessing.
I will bless those who bless you,
and whoever curses you I will curse;
and all peoples on earth
will be blessed through you."

GENESIS 12:1–3 NIV

Though he had stopped short of Canaan earlier, at this point Abram stepped up to lead his family. Now a seventy-five-year-old man, he took his wife, Sarai, his nephew Lot, all their servants and possessions, and began the trek to Canaan. Can you imagine what Sarai's reaction might have been? She is childless, meaning no natural support system within her family, and Abram is saying, "We're relocating again, but I'm not sure where we're going. We will know it when we get there." But this time he obeyed. No doubt it required great courage and resolve.

The farther they got from Haran, the more difficult the trip became. It was dry and dusty with little vegetation. Water was scarce. Imagine how tempting it would have been to linger at an oasis and think, "This is far enough." But Abram had a different mindset this time. He kept going. Eventually they arrived in the new land, and to no one's surprise, it was already inhabited. God was very pleased with Abram's full obedience, and He renewed His promise to Abram, saying, "To your descendants I will give this land." Abram responded by building an altar to the Lord, and another near Bethel as he continued to journey on. Besides deepening his relationship with God, he was making a statement in a world of idol worshippers that he was choosing the one true God, the invisible God who was not to be found in stone or wood images. It appears his confidence was growing as God reaffirmed that He would bless him, along with his cattle, land, family, and name.

Despite the promises of blessings, though, Abram was caught with the rest of the people in a famine so severe Abram apparently forgot

God said He would bless him in that very land. Maybe Sarai and the people he led were asking, "Seriously? You brought us on this long and ridiculous journey for this?" Abram was under great pressure, facing the prospect of losing all his flocks, perhaps even his family and his life. At this point, we don't read, "And Abram called on the Lord." Instead, he took action on his own, and gathered the whole community for a trip to Egypt for help and deliverance.

Acting on your own after God has promised He will lead and guide you? Not giving God the opportunity to show his power and deliverance? Not a good move.

Abram was out of his league in Egypt, and he knew it. He was a nomad, with only his traveling entourage for protection. The Egyptians were powerful and in total control. Sarai was beautiful, and Abram was in "I'll do this myself" mode. He figured life would go better for him in Egypt if the men there thought Sarai was his eligible sister, not his wife. So even though God had taken the initiative in the covenant to bless him, Abram decided this situation was his burden and responsibility. He instructed Sarai to join him in lying about their true relationship. Sure enough, she was the hot new topic right away in Egypt, and since she was apparently free for the taking, Sarai was taken to Pharaoh's palace. Abram, the lucky "brother," was given herds of sheep, oxen, donkeys, camels, and even servants in return.

Almost immediately, though, the deal went sour. God sent trouble to Pharaoh's house because of Sarai, after which the ruler discovered Sarai actually was Abram's wife. Pharaoh was angry and ordered Abram to take his wife and all his possessions and go. Abram had lied and endangered his wife. He had been kicked out of the nation that was hosting him during a famine—less than stellar items on Abram's résumé.

Abram was now a rich man, however. He took all his new possessions, much silver and gold among them (Genesis 13), and returned to the altar he had made near Bethel. The record specifically says there he called on the name of the Lord (v.4). Did he talk to God about his failure in Egypt? Did he question if the covenant was still intact? I know when I mess up, I wonder if everything God has told me is off the table. We aren't privy to Abram's prayer, just that he prayed.

Remember God's command to Abram to leave his land and family? Remember Abram's incomplete obedience when God told him to make a complete break? God clearly knew Terah and Lot would be distractions that would only complicate Abram's life and hurt him. In the new land, Lot's character revealed itself. Their combined possessions and wealth became an issue. Because their herdsmen bickered over ranching rights to the land for their flocks, Abram and Lot decided they needed to separate and create some space. Abram's character revealed itself as well. Abram said, "Let's not have any fighting between us," and offered Lot first pick of the land. Lot unhesitatingly chose what appeared to be the prime grazing area.

Abram's unselfishness caught the Lord's attention. As soon as Lot left, God made one more personal appearance, and gave Abram another promise to believe: "Look around from where you are, to the north and south, to the east and west. All the land that you see I will give to you and your offspring forever. I will make your offspring like the dust of the earth, so that if anyone could count the dust, then your offspring could be counted. Go, walk through the length and breadth of the land, for I am giving it to you" (Genesis 13:14–17 NIV). In obedience to God, Abram moved to Hebron, and built another altar there.

Appearances are often deceptive. Though the land was green and inviting, Lot had chosen a dangerous and wicked place to live. The debauched city of Sodom was there. Lot's choice more deeply engrained him in sin and its accompanying dangers. Anyone who makes sinful people his or her close companions will eventually be disappointed. Kidnappers abducted Lot and his family and stole his possessions. Uncle Abram came to the rescue of his ungrateful nephew. He put his own life on the line and put together an army of 318 trained servants to pursue the kidnappers. They were able to set Lot and his people free, as well as recover all of his goods. Abram also captured some of the enemy and their possessions. The King of Sodom, one of the four warring kings Abram faced, tried to make a deal with him. He said, "Give me back the people, and you can keep all the goods."

Abram wasn't even tempted. He immediately responded, "I swear to GOD, The High God, Creator of Heaven and Earth, this solemn oath, that I'll take nothing from you, not so much as a thread or a shoestring. I'm not going to have you go around saying, 'I made Abram rich.'" Think of it! Abram turned his back on a golden opportunity. He didn't keep the spoils of war, only allowed some of his men to keep their share. If you're keeping score (don't we always?), these two incidents are strong positives for Abram.

Abram's boldness at this point seems fantastic! What can stop him now? Well, second thoughts can be anyone's downfall. Perhaps he wondered what was going to happen now that the kings knew exactly where he was, and he had bested them and then scorned a king's offer. Maybe he wondered how he would survive if his resources ran out, and he had alienated the neighbors. For sure he was afraid he was hearing things, because the promise to multiply his descendants was preposterous in the face of his childlessness. God who knows our hearts and thoughts intimately visited Abram in a vision. The Almighty addressed Abram, saying, "Do not be afraid, Abram. I am your shield, your very great reward" (Genesis 15:1 NIV).

Abram's deepest fear surfaced. He wasn't comforted by the Lord's words. He was still childless, growing older by the day. Humanly speaking, he had cause to doubt the Lord. And doubt he did. In response to God's promise to protect him and provide him with an amazing reward, Abram reverted to the same struggle he had battled his entire adult life. He was childless. The only heir available to him was his lead servant, Eliezer. "Look, God, you have given me no offspring!" Abram exclaimed. He still didn't have the goods for the promise to be fulfilled.

Abram is rightfully named "the father of the faithful," but a case could be made for identifying him as "the father of the unfaithful." If you were keeping score, where would you put Abraham? Look back. Nothing spectacular singled him out from the beginning. His track record is uncertain at best, a roller coaster of ups and downs. He's bold and strong, and then cowering and deceitful. Almighty God promises him...well, promises him the world, actually. And his response is to point out what God hasn't given him yet. God keeps coming back to him, though, so that might push your vote slightly over the "good enough" mark. What do you think? If you were in charge of deciding whom you would make the "father" of your people, has he performed well enough to convince you yet? Or would you keep looking?

For Further Thought

1) What are some things that could make a "not good enough" list in your life? Like Abram, do you lack the "stuff" that typically makes success? Have you been disobedient, or only partially obedient? Have you allowed family members to take precedence over God? Do you tend to be your own savior, acting independently? Are you willing to lie and manipulate to protect yourself and your desires?

2) If you were keeping records on yourself, would you say you have more on the good side of the ledger or on the bad side?

2

"What Do I Still Lack?"
(Matthew 19:20)

Remember this?

Father Abraham had many sons,
Many sons had Father Abraham.
And I am one of them, and so are you,
So let's just praise the Lord!
Right arm! left arm!

If that and the accompanying arm and leg motions don't ring a bell for you, you must not have ever gone to camp or ridden a packed bus for a field trip. That childhood song recognizes the fact that God always keeps His promises. He kept His promise to Abraham to bless him, and make him the Father of many nations. We are all his children in faith. But before we think any more about Abram/Abraham and what made him good enough for God, let's consider a couple of Abram's children.

He was probably known as Joseph or Peter or Matthew or Gad or Aaron—certainly by a good Jewish name. Let's call him Aaron. That would make him the namesake of the first high priest, brother of Moses. That's a name any true Jewish man would be proud to carry. Matthew, Mark, and Luke all call him the "rich young ruler" (Matthew 19:16–22, Mark 10:17–27, Luke 18:18–20).

"Ruler" means that Aaron was a Pharisee. Because of all the bad press the Pharisees got from the majority's response to Jesus, we tend to assume that being a Pharisee was a bad thing. But "Pharisee" simply designated the religious group with which he was identified. Nicodemus, the ruler who came to Jesus at night to discuss spiritual things, then later stood up for Jesus when He was being tried, was a Pharisee. As a Pharisee and ruler, Aaron was a leader in one of the local synagogues. Scholars say there were about 480 synagogues in Jerusalem in Aaron's time, in addition to the large temple in Jerusalem. The synagogues were smaller neighborhood gatherings for the Jews. The word "synagogue" actually means "meeting place." The synagogue served as the social center where the Jews in the neighborhood gathered. It was the educational venue for keeping the law before the people, and for providing instruction for their children. It was the substitute place for temple worship, precluded for many on a regular basis by distance or poverty. The study of the law in the synagogues took the place of sacrifices until the yearly trek when all worshippers went to the Temple. The synagogues were vital to the life of faithful Jews. Jesus Himself went regularly to the synagogue.

We might call Aaron "the head deacon." He actually was the chief lay administrative officer for the synagogue. He was in the position because he was well respected. His life had earned him that place. He was upright, known for his integrity. Because Aaron was a good Pharisee, he knew the Old Testament front and back, up and down, and all around. Nothing in the scrolls eluded him. He was well versed in the Law of Moses and could quote the Ten Commandments word for word with his eyes closed. He knew every recorded prophecy about the Messiah. His knowledge and ability were impressive.

Aaron's record and performance were impeccable. After all, he was a Pharisee, right? The Pharisees were fixated on piety and keeping the law. They feared nothing more than breaking one of the commandments. To make sure they would not go astray, they built a fence of sorts around the commandments. They added 248 more commandments and then 365 lesser prohibitions to their code of conduct to ensure they did not even approach violating the original ten. That would be akin to being so afraid of breaking the 50 mph speed limit on the road near your home that you installed a regulator on your car that won't let you go past 10 mph.

All those rules made Aaron a moral straight arrow. When there was gossip in the community, it wasn't about him. Everyone knew that Aaron was, as the elder women commented with pride, "as good as they come." He gave to the poor, helped the weak, and generally was a credit to his family name. He was the one mothers used as a motivational example to their own less than remarkable sons. "Why can't you be more like Aaron?"

He was young, meaning he was somewhere from his early twenties to perhaps forty years of age. Apparently he had achieved his religious and community stature in a remarkably short amount of time. When people noted that he was the ruler of the synagogue, they always pointed out his comparative youth. You know how that is. We talk about someone being "so mature for their age," or "wiser than their years." That was Aaron.

If that wasn't enough, Aaron was rich. He had silver and gold, cattle, sheep, houses, land, and property; he had many and great possessions. Whatever he needed, he could obtain. Whatever he wanted, the resources were his for the using. A rich young ruler. Possessions, power, prestige, and a good stretch of life likely yet before him. A guy like that surely laid his head on the pillow at night fully satisfied and content. Someone in his position would jump out of bed in the morning filled with confidence and purpose, right?

Not so much. Though he had all of this

to his credit, Aaron was strangely empty and dissatisfied. He knew that compared to most everyone he knew, he was good. Flat out good. His performance was on his mind every day. He went to bed at night, mentally checking off the long list to make sure where he stood. But something about him didn't feel quite settled. Was he good enough? Good enough to receive eternal life? Good enough for God?

There was a rabbi in the area who was attracting the attention of the poor common people clear up through the religious elite. He was different. He was someone even Aaron considered holy and good, way above the norm. God's hand was obviously on this man named Jesus, for He was even performing miracles. Everyone knew that no one could do the things Jesus did unless God was with him. He was the topic of conversation in every synagogue around Jerusalem. Jesus from Nazareth was the most promising candidate to ever come along to help Aaron settle his unease and answer his question.

So Aaron sought an opportunity. Jesus was with His disciples, and Aaron ran up to Him, knelt, and in front of everyone, got right to the point. No polite and careful easing into a personal conversation. "Good Master," he said, "What do I need to do to be sure of eternal life? To be good enough for God?" "Good Master" was not an unusual way to address a religious teacher. Aaron could have called Nicodemus Good Master or any member of the Sanhedrin, a ruling body of twenty to twenty-three respected Pharisees in every city. It was similar to respectfully calling Jesus Good Teacher.

Have you ever asked a simple, sincere question, and then been flabbergasted by a question in return? Aaron was, because Jesus answered his question with a question. "Why do you evaluate Me as good?" Jesus said no one was truly good but God. If Aaron was simply trying to be polite, if he was flattering Jesus, or if he was showing simple respect, it didn't influence Jesus at all. While Aaron fished around for an appropriate answer, Jesus continued. "If you feel like you have to do something, keep the commandments."

Since Aaron was a Pharisee, he had this one in the bag. But maybe there was something else.

Another question. "Which commandments?" he asked.

Jesus counted on his fingers, "You know. Do not murder. Don't commit adultery. Don't steal. Don't lie." He continued, "Honor your mother and father, love your neighbor as yourself."

"Yes, yes. Those I know." Aaron interrupted. "I have kept all of those as long as I can remember." It was true. He had never wanted another man's wife, let alone slept with her. He wouldn't keep a stalk of grain that wasn't his. He adored his parents, and he was meticulously honest. Everyone knew he was generous to a fault. Truly speaking, though he would never say it aloud, he really was a fine man, one of the best anyone could know. Being as honest as he could be in his own heart, he knew he had kept the law as well as his sainted father. If that really was what it took to be good enough, his bases were covered. So why wasn't he 100 percent sure? Why was he still so unsettled? Why couldn't he lay this question to rest?

"Those I have kept, Jesus. All of them. What is it that I lack? Where am I missing the standard?"

Jesus read Aaron like the proverbial book.

He knew that Aaron's confidence was in his performance. He knew Aaron was proud of the way he compared with the rest of the people. You know, the sinners. So Jesus spoke to Aaron in his own language, words He knew would slice straight to the heart of his reasoning. "You think you need to do something? You want to perform perfectly? All right then. Here's what it will take for you. Sell everything you have—all your many possessions. Give the proceeds away to charitable causes to care for the poor and destitute. Divest yourself of your property, your possessions, and your safety net. When you have let go of it all, come follow Me."

Aaron was stunned. The sleeve of his purple and white robe trembled as he raised his hand to his mouth and cleared his throat. "I'm sorry. . . You said. . . ?" Surely the rabbi could see, surely He knew Aaron's reputation. Aaron was a better man than every one of this teacher's disciples. Jesus knew it. He hadn't argued with him about his performance on the commandments. He knew all Aaron had claimed was true.

Jesus looked back with a slight smile. "Aaron," He repeated firmly and compassionately, "If perfect performance is your desire, sell everything you have. Let go of all the proceeds. Give it all away." He saw Aaron wince. "Give all the proceeds to the poor. Then come follow Me."

The disciples had stopped talking when Aaron first started the conversation. They wondered what a synagogue ruler, a Pharisee, wanted with Jesus. He was far above them in status and reputation. Since he clearly had such respect for Jesus, maybe the rabbi would invite him to follow as well. Maybe this addition of a well-known, highly respected good guy would help Jesus and the message finally be accepted. He had resources, at least, and God knew they could use those. He was easily a better specimen than any of them. So what was Jesus doing? They were amazed and bewildered.

So was Aaron. Disbelieving and sad, he wordlessly backed away from the rabbi. Apparently he had given the teacher too much credit. He came to Jesus sincerely, asking for clarification on what would make him good enough, looking for guidance on anything he might have overlooked. The man told him to do something that was unreasonable, something that was not even a commandment. Aaron already kept the commandments better than Jesus' disciples. Job, Abraham, and many of the revered men of God in Jewish history had been rich. They didn't have to give away their wealth to be good enough. What was up with this?

For centuries Jesus' reply to the rich young ruler's question has baffled New Testament readers. What *was* the rich young ruler saying about being good enough for God? Good enough for heaven and eternal life? If near perfect performance, far and away better than 99 percent of the people, isn't enough, who then can be? The disciples asked the question immediately. "If this perfect specimen doesn't meet the standard, will anyone ever?"

What do you think? If you are keeping score, how does Aaron rate? Far more pluses than minuses? If you were in charge of managing the "good enough" standard, would he get the nod?

For Further Thought:

1) Every society and culture has standards for behavior, basic minimum requirements that separate the good from the bad. Then there are extraordinary characteristics and actions that make a person outstanding. In your family, church, and circle of acquaintances, what are the items on the checklists? What must you avoid at all costs?

2) Based on those standards, how do you rate?

3) In what areas do you have a tendency to compare yourself with others?

3

"Lord, Remember Me" (Luke 23:42)

———————

According to much tradition and the apocryphal book The Gospel of Nicodemus, his name was Dismas. Dismas was a name taken from the Greek word for "sunset" or "death." If that truly was his name, he was not from Jewish lineage. He may have been of mixed parentage, perhaps a Roman citizen. Maybe his parents named him with a sense of foreboding or even a premonition about his future. Maybe they simply didn't want him. Throughout history, names are given most commonly to honor someone, or to signify the hopes for the child being named. Who would name a child "death" or "sunset"? We get the word "dismal" from the same root.

Maybe that name affected the young child. Maybe every time someone said his name, it triggered memories of clear disappointment in the eyes of his mother. Maybe it reminded him of the lack of investment from his father. Perhaps Dismas got teased about his name. Maybe they called him "Dead Boy" or "Walking Death." Maybe they taunted him and said, "Yeah, the sun has gone down on you, buddy. It's dark! Your day is over." You know how merciless kids can be. If it's true that our childhood experiences and family choices/history shape us for good or evil (generational curses and blessings: biblical evidence for this in Exodus 18, 30, 24, and 36; Leviticus 26; Numbers 14; Deuteronomy 5, 24, 28, 30; Psalm 103), Dismas must have gotten a bad start. Maybe he was abused. Poor. Alone.

As it is for all of us, however, eventually, regardless of our start in life, we become responsible for our choices. Children and even teenagers can be excused for many things, but adults are held responsible for their own lives. By the time we are in our midtwenties, certainly by thirty, we are where we are because of our own choices. Dismas started making choices that were his own, and it took him down dark and dangerous paths.

John 19, Mark 15, and Matthew 27 all mention his shameful end, but Luke focuses on him and tells a more complete story. John's account calls Dismas a thief or a robber, but most scholars agree it is a weak translation. The most accurate translation is Luke's choice of the word *malefactor*. Malefactor means more than simple thievery, more than just taking what was not yours. It was a word usually reserved for the more heinous, serious evildoers. And that's what Dismas became.

At some point, Dismas decided that what he desired and deserved in life was not going to come through normal channels, or that the approved way of getting there was too difficult. He became the master of the shortcut, taking what he wanted when he wanted it, regardless of who got hurt. Slowly but inevitably it became a way of life. Though he refused to pay the price for possessions and power others did, he paid for it in other ways. Little by little he was rejected by the lovely girl who captured his interest and heart. He was isolated from any true friends, and his hard heart insulated him from caring, too. Oh, he had moments of regret, but that was it. Just fleeting moments, and he was soon back at it with an even more calloused attitude. When he first began lying and stealing as a way of life instead of simply to survive, he thought that would be it. But the first day he had to kill a man who fought back when Dismas attacked the traveler in the desert to rob him, he was surprised that it didn't really bother him. For a long time, he had made his home in the caves and rocks alongside the isolated patch road where travelers had to pass between Jerusalem and Jericho. When a lone journeyer or small group of travelers came by, he would swoop down on them, killing some outright, and leaving others for dead while he ransacked their possessions, keeping all the loot. He had left wailing infants to perish unprotected, and beaten into submission older people who tried to escape and find help.

But this way of life had caught up with the highwayman. Someone had recognized him, and the soldiers captured Dismas, dragging him, cursing and kicking, from his cave. Another man, as degenerate as Dismas, was taken into custody near the same time. They were both put in prison after a speedy, uncontested trial.

Death was the sentence. Romans typically didn't sentence anyone to imprisonment unless they were awaiting another trial. Instead, they would be killed, or sentenced to the harshest of work, chained in the salt mines for a lifetime, or given a life sentence as a galley slave. The only Jews typically punished by the Roman government were those who had committed a crime against Rome. If the evil was done to one of their own people, Rome told the Jews to handle it. Galley and salt mine slaves were free labor, so that was the common punishment for evil-doing Roman citizens. Life was hard and cheap for those punished in this way, but the soldiers took good enough care of the prisoners to assure the work was done or the voyage accomplished. Crucifixion was horrendous, so much so that it was generally prohibited in the case of Roman citizens, reserved only for the worst of the worst.

That was Dismas and the other man. They were in prison briefly, waiting for the next scheduled time of crucifixion. The prison for such criminals was subterranean, dug into rock underground. Dismas was lowered into an opening the size of a manhole, the only way in or out of the prison. The stench caused him to gag while he was still attached to the rope on the way down. Maybe this was worse than death. Dirt, debris, feces mingled with the darkness and overcame him.

He didn't know how long he was there because day and night were exactly the same in this hole of darkness, no light or conversation or hope. Only the moans of other wretches could be heard, the barest outlines of a huddled human glimpsed occasionally through narrowed eyes. Rain leaked through the dirt and rock above him a time or two, and he didn't even try to work his chains free enough to avoid it.

But today a soldier was lowered through the hole, and he gruffly grabbed first the other man, and shoved him toward the opening. The criminal could hardly move and he weakly tried to take a swing at the soldier as he cursed the centurion loudly. The Roman guard cuffed him about the head, attached the rope around his arms, and they pulled him up. Then it was Dismas's turn. He was too weak to resist, so the soldiers easily pulled him up and dropped him on the ground. "On your feet," the tallest helmeted man commanded. "This is it." Blinking and trying to shield his eyes from the blinding sunlight, Dismas tried to obey.

The next hour or so was a painful blur. He was in so much agony he didn't know how much time had passed. But he ended up on a hill outside Jerusalem. It was a craggy, rocky location everyone knew. And it was a scary place. He remembered when he was young, this was the place the adults used to threaten the children, trying to curb their misbehaving. "The soldiers will take you to Golgotha if you aren't careful!" And now, here he was. He, the other desperado who had been in the hole, and another man Dismas did not recognize.

As the soldiers were making their preparations for the gruesome task of crucifying three men, the other criminal was yelling obscenities at the crowd gathered to witness the spectacle. It was entertainment of the most warped kind, and entire families were there to witness the gory details. Dismas was having a near out-of-body experience watching it all. It was surreal that he was here. Here like this.

Then there was the other man. He had been

badly beaten, strips of bloody skin hanging from His back. A crown crudely constructed from huge thorn branches was pressed into His forehead and hair, leaving trails of oozing blood through tangled and matted hair, streaming around His nose and dripping from His chin. Other than hoarse and racking sounds as He breathed, He was silent. A group of weeping women who looked genteel and good was gathered near Him, shuddering with the horror of what was happening to Him. A young man, disbelief and horror darkening his eyes, hovered protectively over one dark-haired woman, bowed nearly to the ground in her grief. The man they called Jesus turned to them and in a strangely commanding voice said, "My daughters, don't weep for me. Weep for yourselves. Hard days are coming."

The soldiers made placards on parchment to nail on the cross above the head of each man, listing the crimes committed. The writing was in Greek, Latin, and Hebrew as an understandable and horrific warning to everyone who passed: do these crimes, and this is what will happen to you. His and the other criminal's list was so vile that women blushed and men spat toward them. But that other man. No terrible crimes were listed above His head. Even in his own anguish Dismas couldn't get past it. It simply said, "This is the King of the Jews." For this He was being crucified? A death reserved for the most egregious criminals?

Soon the actual crucifixion began. Crucifixion was intended to provide a death that was particularly slow, painful (hence the term excruciating, literally "out of crucifying"), gruesome, humiliating, and public. It was not just an execution; it was a humiliation, stripping the victim, making him as vulnerable as possible, subjecting him to jests and mockery. Despite its frequent use by the Romans, many of the thinkers of the day were like Cicero, who described it as a "most cruel and disgusting punishment." Both criminals were stretched out on their crosses, mallets thudding, the sounds of breaking bones in hands and feet mingling with their blood-curdling screams. Then it was Jesus' turn. Dismas was more shocked by the man's reaction as they nailed Him to the cross in the center than he was by his own pain. No cursing, just deep, agonized groans. He clearly was restraining Himself from giving full vent to His torment, and it seemed to be an effort to protect the women. They dropped the cross into the hole. Jesus' body jerked, convulsed with pain, and then He looked heavenward and said in a clear, distinct voice, "Father, forgive them. They don't realize what they are doing." What? They certainly did know what they were doing. They enjoyed it, too.

In the next hours as the three men hung separately, yet together, Dismas learned much about the man on the middle cross. The soldiers and the crowd alike mocked Him. They said Jesus claimed to be the chosen Messiah of God, the Son of God Himself. They remembered miracles He had performed, kindnesses He had shown. They reminisced about His purity, how He preached a gospel of love. Some told of how He had literally saved their lives. Others made fun of Him and said, "Isn't this ironic? He saved others, but is powerless to save Himself. Some Messiah He is!"

The soldiers were bored. They had done this many times. When Jesus was thirsty, they poured vinegar onto an old dirty sponge, and lifted it on the tip of a spear for Him to drink. "If You are King of the Jews," they laughed, "save Yourself!" Jesus just looked at them, and Dismas felt like he could see compassion in His eyes. Maybe it was the hot sun. Maybe it was his pain. Maybe he was delirious, but it seemed to him the man on the cross was more in control than His executioners.

Dismas discovered the older woman he had especially noticed was Jesus' mother. The young man seemed to be a very close friend. Jesus pushed through His intense pain to lovingly direct them to care for one another. He told the young man to take His mother as that man's own. It was incredible. Maybe this man was the Messiah. He certainly was made of different stuff than Dismas was. Different than the religious people he had always despised. The hatred the religious people in the crowd displayed for Jesus, and their delight in seeing His pain had to be provoked by something entirely different than they represented. Different than anything he had ever seen or imagined.

The other criminal cursed and spewed the most vulgar profanities every time he gathered enough strength to do so. He eventually turned his attention from the crowd and the soldiers to Jesus. He described Jesus in unthinkable, unspeakable terms, and then derided, "If You are the Christ sent from God, if You are the Savior, crawl down off this cross! Save Yourself and us!"

Dismas couldn't take it any longer. He blurted out, "Stop! Do you not even have any respect for God, or fear of Him? We, you and I, are experiencing this worst of all deaths because we deserve it! Our wickedness has brought us to this place. Our punishment is justice—exactly as it should be. This is what the law promises sinners and criminals like us will get. We are beyond repair. But this man—this man has done nothing wrong."

Overwhelmed by that realization, Dismas turned his head with hope and pleaded to the man on the center cross. "Lord, I know You are headed for Your Kingdom. When you get there, please. . . please remember me!"

Seriously? Did he really say that? Did he expect that? Dismas was somewhere between thirty and sixty years old. Did he expect two short sentences, just words, to make up for years of debauchery and villainy? He had lived like the devil. He admitted he was getting exactly what he deserved. He will be dead, the last ounce of life drained from him, before sundown. Jesus has been preaching, "Repent and be baptized." How is that going to happen? Jesus told everyone who followed Him to produce fruits that evidenced their repentance. Dismas had no chance to do anything good. He's asking now for some special favor, to be remembered in this King's kingdom?

Ridiculous, right? If you had to decide, how would you handle Dismas? A rap sheet as long as your arm, vicious and vile living opposed to maybe a dozen words he has no opportunity to prove. Is he good enough?

For Further Thought:

1) Is there anything you think might forever disqualify someone from receiving God's grace? Can a person go too far to ever recover and be good enough?

2) What are the things in your life you have feared might be unforgiveable?

4

"For Your Sake He Became Poor"
(2 Corinthians 8:9)

Though God had assured ordinary Abram that he was indeed chosen by God for great reward and that he would have many descendants, Abram couldn't fathom it. In his day, a childless man's estate would go to his lead servant, so Abram's servant Eliezer would be the designated heir. Abram found this circumstance crushing. God had told him several times, up close and personal, that Abram would indeed be the father of not just one child, but of many. Years into these conversations, God came to talk to Abram again, and gave the same message (Genesis 15). Right in the middle of God's assurances, Abram interrupted, "Look, you have given me no children! A mere house servant is going to get everything I have!"

Humanly speaking, it is easy to sympathize with Abram. It seems ludicrous that God would keep talking about many descendants when Sarai and Abram were well past typical childbearing years, no child in sight. Abram was aching for a single son; God was thinking about nations. God heard Abram's confusion and anguish and said, "No, Eliezer will not be your heir. You're going to have someone to follow you who will come from your own body."

Then He took Abram outside underneath the night sky. "Look up!" He said. "Can you count those stars? You know you can't. And that's how your descendants will eventually be—too many to count." And something amazing happened. Abram believed! God promised and Abram believed! Genesis 15:6 (NIV) says, "Abram believed the LORD, and he credited it to him as righteousness." The Hebrew word for believed means to say "Amen!" or "let it be so." God gave a promise, and in faith the very ordinary, not spectacular, "not good enough" Abram responded in faith. God initiated contact, made a promise, and Abram took the leap of faith. He believed it.

God's response to Abram's faith was more astounding than Abram's faith by far. Though Abram had been slow to believe, and even slower to fully obey, when he took the leap and responded in faith, God "credited it to him as righteousness." This action on God's part was so amazing that centuries later, the apostle Paul used this very account to explain to the Christians in Rome how God's heart is always turned toward those "not good enough," and they become justified and made righteous in His eyes when they believe.

Obviously, Abram could not clearly understand the full meaning of what God had said. The eternal implications passed by him, and he wasn't totally clear even what it meant for him in the here and now. Whatever his understanding at this point in time, we know that his choice to believe what God had said was transformative. God saw it as righteousness, and Abram began to grow in faith. The writer of Hebrews reflects on Abram's life as faith- and purpose-filled: "By faith he [Abraham] lived as an alien in the land of promise, as in a foreign land, dwelling in tents with Isaac and Jacob, fellows heirs of the same promise; for he was looking for the city which has foundations, whose architect and builder is God" (Hebrews 11:9–10 NASB).

Thinking back through Abram's journey to this point, we can see ourselves and our own experiences, and we begin to make sense of the path. First, God did not choose Abram because he was especially worthy, born for success, or any of the qualifiers we might expect. Jim Collins, one of this decade's best thinkers and writers, says for a business or venture to succeed, a leader needs to have "the right person in the right seat on the bus." And that is true even in this place. God needed the right person to be in the right place, one who would choose to believe Him. Our selection by God is not because we are so outstanding. It is because God sees us and loves us.

God is the prime mover. Abram didn't wake up one day and say out of the blue, "I'm turning over a new leaf. I believe I will make the rest of my life the best of my life. I am going to impress God and perhaps He will give me a great reward." God was thinking of Abraham before Abraham gave God any notice. God saw him way back in the pagan community, where virtually everyone had given up faith and belief in the one true God, the Almighty about whom Noah had spoken. God saw Abram, wanted to be his friend and use him in a powerful way. So, God initiated the contact with Abram. That is just what He does with us.

We often mis-state and confuse the truth when we say things like, "I found God." Understandable, because when we are spiritually blind, God can be right in front of us, His presence visible to everyone else around us, and we don't have a clue that He is there. Jeremiah says that when we seek Him, we will always find Him, because He wants to know us. In *I Will Be Found By You*, Francis Frangipane writes, "I believe that the real goal of Christianity is not to create a religion about God but that we would actually know Him." That certainly is God's goal for us. That is why He is the initiator. Just as He came to Abram and called him out while he was living life with the pagans, God comes to us where we are. He picks us to have a relationship with Him even before we know enough to recognize or value Him.

As with Abram, rarely do we pick up and

obediently follow God the first time He calls to us. Like Abram, we are influenced by our surroundings and the people close to us, controlled by our fears, and we make partial moves. Sometimes we are so slow that people who are watching us see no movement toward God or spiritual interest at all. It's imperceptible, except to God. Our loving, pursuing Father keeps coming back to us. Genesis records God coming to Abram with the call and the promise at least three times before he actually believed God. But God kept giving him opportunities for faith.

How about you? Can you look back over your life and see inroads God made with you before you truly believed Him? I believed God and my faith was counted to me for righteousness when I was sixteen years old, a junior in high school. A moment on that day sealed the deal for me, but there were many times prior in my life that God had shown Himself to me. He was the prime mover. He was and still is the initiator.

Aristotle became famous for his metaphysical arguments. He believed that all movement depends on there being a mover at the start. For Aristotle, movement meant more than something traveling. Movement also included change, growth, melting, cooling, and heating. Aristotle recognized that everything in the world is in a state of flux.

Aristotle argued that behind every movement there must be a chain of events that brought about the movement that we see taking place. He argued that this chain of events must lead back to something which moves, but is itself unmoved and unchanging. This is referred to as the Prime Mover. That is how he explained Creation. That is also the best description of how spiritual life, growth, and change occur. Mankind never makes the first move toward God. Abram didn't, no biblical hero did, and I didn't—no one in history has initiated his own relationship with God. He initiates contact every single time. He is unchanging. "I the LORD do not change" (Malachi 3:6 NIV).

That is the most amazing message of the Gospel of good news. Jesus spoke it plainly, "I have come to seek and to save the lost" (Luke 19:10 NIV). 2 Peter 3:9 reminds us that God doesn't want anyone to perish, anyone to lack a relationship with Him. So He initiates. He calls, He draws,

He comes looking for us as He did for Abraham. Like Abram, we have a choice.

Some of us have a hard time with that, because it seems that human beings are so different. Some of us are insulted by the term "lost." We are too sophisticated, too educated, and too good to be lost. Sure, we could probably improve a little, who couldn't? But we are decidedly not lost or hopeless.

We have similar difficulty thinking of ourselves as spiritually poor. But when Jesus announced His mission here, the reason why He came, He said, "The Spirit of the Lord is upon me to preach the good news to the poor" (Luke 4:18, quoting Isaiah 61:1). Jesus didn't say, "I am coming to preach good news, to the poor also." He said plain and simple, "I am proclaiming good news to the poor." Period.

The Gospel is the good news that God rescues and saves the poor. The only target group for the good news is the spiritually poor, those who have nothing good enough to offer God, and they know it. In the days when Jesus walked the earth in human flesh, the poor, wretched, and miserable were the ones who welcomed Him most gladly.

The parables Jesus told to spotlight the power of God always feature those who have nothing. Like a child, they have nothing to offer, nothing to bring. They just come to Jesus and believe.

The rich young ruler, also known as Aaron—his problem was that he wasn't poor enough to believe. He felt like he had the goods, the resources. He believed where he was in life was his own doing, and that whatever else was needed, he could provide or perform. So he refused God's call. Dismas, the criminal on the cross, was so very poor. Among our very last possessions is life. His was waning by the second; he had no chance to turn over a new leaf, to set a new track record, or to do anything of redeeming worth. He had absolutely nothing to offer, nothing of his own to commend him. He just believed God, and, just as with his father Abram, it was "counted to him for righteousness."

God came looking for Adam and Eve in the garden, not to punish them, but to fellowship with them. God came looking for Abram to be his friend and fulfill a mammoth promise. Jesus Christ initiated contact with the spiritually poor, not to chastise us and point out our failures, but to bring us into His family and kingdom. The Gospel is only for the poor. The good news is only for sinners. And we are all sinners, poor, lost, and far from God. Our poverty puts every son of Adam, every daughter of Eve, on equal footing.

Jesus' entire purpose and mission is summed up in these simple words: "For you know the grace of our Lord Jesus Christ, that though he was rich, yet for your sake he became poor, so that you through his poverty might become rich" (2 Corinthians 8:9 NIV). Jesus became spiritually poor. His own Father turned away from Him on the cross because of the sins of the world He carried, in order to pay the price for our sins. God says when we believe that by faith, and act on it by accepting His sacrifice, we who could never be good enough for God, become righteous in His sight, because He views us through Jesus Christ.

Abram could never have been good enough for God, good enough to be chosen by God. But because of His heart for sinners like us, God chooses us anyway, despite our lack of merit. We become good enough for God by believing Him, acting on our faith. The apostle Paul discovered this truth in a dynamic, up-close-and-personal encounter with the God who was pursuing him. Let's look at his story and see how it overlaps with Abraham's.

For Further Thought:

Draw a time line, with the line going before and after your birth, right up to where you are today. What events can you mark on the line, before you were even born, that evidence God pursuing you, setting up a way for you to know Him? Mark all the significant events or people He brings to your mind, right up until the moment you believed God, and He made you "good enough." If you have not yet begun this remarkable journey and are still spiritually poor, mark today on the line as another event where God is pursuing you. He made sure you got this book in order to "find Him."

5

"Who Are You, Lord?" (Acts 9:5)

────────

Saul was born to a Jewish mother, and raised Jewish, though his father must have been a Roman citizen. Saul was a citizen of Rome, and it had to come from his father's side, because Romans didn't recognize parental citizenship from a mother. Perhaps his father was a Gentile who converted to Judaism. In any case, Saul was raised a Jew and no one ever carried the title with more pride. As a young boy, his parents were sure to give him the best they could offer. He was educated at the feet of Gamaliel, one of the most famous Jewish teachers and a member of the Sanhedrin. He had the privileges of birth and position, and Saul took them to heart.

Growing up as a devout Jewish boy, one who had the best education and indoctrination available to him, Saul was totally and thoroughly convinced he was right. He was ready and eager to answer any challenges to his faith, with physical action, if required. The rabbi from Nazareth gathered quite a following of mostly ordinary, scantily educated, and often impoverished Jews before His crucifixion for blasphemy. Saul had never met Him, and was disgusted by the feverish, inexplicable loyalty of so many to a dead man. How could they forsake their own families, traditions, and heritage for someone who ended in such a shameful manner, let alone made the incredulous claims of Jesus? True, they claimed He came back to life again, but honestly? Even unschooled children knew that was impossible.

Saul eventually had close experience with these followers. Supposedly great miracles were happening among them, and it was becoming a fad to attend their gatherings. "You know how the mob mentality grows," Saul thought, when he heard that quite a number of temple priests had joined the rapidly growing group in Jerusalem. "I need to see this for myself," he decided, and he went to see a local Christ follower named Stephen, who was hauled before the Sanhedrin to testify. The mob of the Jewish faithful was really angry with Stephen. They presented the high priest with a long list of blasphemies Stephen had supposedly committed.

To his own consternation, Saul felt reluctant respect for the man as he spoke. He wasn't belligerent; he clearly honored the high priest, and gave a measured, systematic, and entirely accurate summary of Jewish history. Stephen traced Yahweh's dealings with mankind, the Jews in particular, from the time of Abraham right up to that moment. He didn't overlook the rebellion and disobedience of their ancestors, and then he made the fatal mistake. He told the mob that they, too, were rebellious and disobedient! He said they mistreated and killed the prophets who told that the Righteous One, the Messiah, was coming. Then, over their shouted objections, he continued, "And when the Messiah they prophesied came, Jesus the Christ, you murdered Him, too! You received the law that was given through angels, and you disobeyed it!"

Saul knew this was trouble. As much as he was

in awe of the man's courage, he was angry. Stephen was accusing him, too. The men in the Sanhedrin rose up with vengeance and rage in their eyes. They rushed at Stephen, and he simply raised his eyes to heaven and called out with urgency, "Look! I see heaven open! And there he is—Jesus standing at the right hand of God, His Father!"

This was too much. The men threw off their coats, and threw them toward Saul. He grabbed the coats and held the garments for them as they dragged Stephen into the street, and began to pummel him with stones. With blood streaming from his skull, his chest heaving from multiple blows, Stephen said words that burned themselves into Saul's soul, "Lord, don't hold this sin against these men! Receive my spirit!" And then he was dead. It was over.

Saul didn't stay to see what they did with the body. He was troubled. This was not what he came to see. The man's clear eyes, respectful tone, and absolute confidence in the reality of someone Saul could not see had shaken him. What was it with these people? He couldn't explain it.

Have you noticed that often what we can't

explain we try to destroy? That's what happened with Saul. He approved of the killing. It was the logical end result. Stephen should have known better. He asked for exactly what he got. Many people felt the same way, and a great persecution broke out against the Christ-followers in Jerusalem. They scattered, fleeing Jerusalem for Judea and Samaria. But they couldn't escape Saul's flaming rage. He made it his business to see that this nonsense was stopped once and for all. He went from house to house, dragging the Christian men and women into the streets for public humiliation, beating, and imprisonment.

The mission consumed him. It was the first thing he thought of in the morning and the last thought he had as he drifted to sleep at night. He would stop this. He would give his time and energy and resources to do it. He wasn't satisfied with the havoc and destruction he had rained down on Jerusalem. Saul went to the high priest and asked for traveling papers to take to the city of Damascus, arrest and imprison anyone he found presumptuous enough to still follow this Jesus.

Papers in hand, a band of men with him,

Saul headed for that city. As he came into the town, a bright light flashed around him. Actually, the light accosted him! He was mentally and physically knocked off balance. Saul actually fell off his horse, instantly discerning he was in the presence of someone terrifyingly powerful, who was speaking directly to him. "Saul! Saul!" the voice urgently called from the brilliance. "Why are you persecuting me?"

Trembling and astonished, Saul asked, "Who are you, Lord?" He called the person he couldn't see "Lord," because he believed he knew the answer without being told.

He was right. "I am Jesus, the one you are persecuting."

Just like that, Saul believed. When Jesus told Saul, now physically blind from his spiritually illuminating experience, to go into the city of Damascus and submit himself to an unknown man Saul had originally come to persecute, Saul did it. Jesus went ahead of Saul in a vision and introduced him to Ananias, the Christian leader Saul was going to meet. Ananias had heard all the horrifying facts about Saul, the violent persecutor.

But Jesus identified Saul to him as "my chosen instrument to proclaim my name to the Gentiles and their kings and to the people of Israel." What? What could Saul have possibly done in three days since the smack down on the Damascus Road to make Jesus believe in him like that?

Nothing. It wasn't what he did. It was what and, more specifically, whom he believed. He believed Jesus, and that was enough. It was enough for Jesus to choose him, it was enough for Ananias to accept him, and it was enough for Saul to move forward in faith in a changed life. In a matter of days, his sight was restored, he was baptized in the name of Jesus, and he began preaching. . .yes, preaching, that Jesus was the Son of God. People were flabbergasted. "What is happening here? This is the man who caused such terror in Jerusalem, and he came here to duplicate it!"

Saul quickly became more and more popular and powerful as he preached that Jesus was in fact God. The Jews concocted a plot to kill Saul. He escaped and went back to Jerusalem, and preached boldly there, too. When he became a target of the Jews he once had served alongside there, too, the believers sent him to Tarsus for his safety. Incredible. The man who once was persecuting followers of Jesus was a follower himself! And Jesus had selected him as a chosen instrument!

How was that possible? It was because when Saul believed the Voice, accepted that this was Jesus, and began to obediently follow Him, God did for Saul what this Jewish boy knew God had done for Abraham. He had learned the story inside out and could tell it word for word. "Abram believed the LORD, and he credited it to him as righteousness" (Genesis 15:6 NIV). Abram wasn't good enough in himself for the standards of a holy God, but God saw his choice to believe, and counted it as righteousness.

That's what happened for Saul. He certainly was not good enough for God. His self-description is condemning—he declared that he was a persecutor (1 Corinthians 15:9), a blasphemer, an injurer, an unbeliever, and the chief of sinners (1 Timothy 1:12–15). In that flash of light, strong conviction, and Almighty Voice, Saul made the choice—"I believe," and then he got up from the ground to put his entire life behind his choice. God responded by viewing him as "good enough."

As the "chosen instrument" of Jesus, his name was changed to Paul. He willingly left home, friends, country, and the future that his great education had created for him. He left all the earthly things that we typically prize and moved in the power of God alone. It was not easy. His sufferings were unparalleled. Deuteronomy's law (25:1–3) specified that no more than 40 lashes were to be given to a criminal. The Jews were careful not to break the smallest laws, so they stopped at 39 stripes with the whip, in case they had miscounted. Paul received from the Jews this punishment on five occasions; he was beaten with rods three times, he was stoned once, he was shipwrecked three times, and he spent a night and a day in the deep. Paul described his additional suffering in this manner: "I suffered the results of many long journeys, and perils of water, perils of robbers, perils by my own countrymen, perils by the heathen, perils in the cities, perils in the wilderness, perils in the sea, perils among false brothers, in weariness, in hunger and thirst, in fastings, and in cold and nakedness, and in the care of all the churches (2 Corinthians 11:23–28 NIV).

Paul's Jewish contemporaries declared that this man who was once their trophy was unworthy of respect. His physical presence was weak and unimpressive, and his speech contemptible and inferior (2 Corinthians 10:10). He had a "thorn in the flesh," a colloquialism used to describe a chronic infirmity, annoyance, or trouble, that worked to keep him humble (2 Corinthians 12:1–11). There was not much about his résumé that would ever have convinced a casual observer he was good enough to lead a great organization, let alone acceptable to the maker of heaven and earth.

Yet he was. Because of properly placed faith, Jesus made Saul/Paul good enough for God. God used him powerfully in his own day, and then the many letters he wrote to the believers in the churches he planted across the known world were preserved over centuries. They became the bulk of the New Testament, which has been the manual for a relationship with God over several thousand years, for millions of people in every imaginable kind of culture. Wycliffe Bible Translators tell us that as of 2013, the entire New Testament has been translated into 1,294 language groups in their "heart language" or native tongue, representing 598 million people.

Paul became a missionary who worked tirelessly to plant churches in major cities all over the Mediterranean. In Acts, we find Paul preaching the Gospel in major cities, then planting churches in a circle or arc from Jerusalem all the way to Illyricum (Romans 15:19). This is a huge area, from Jerusalem circling clear around the coast to what we would call Albania today, just northeast of Italy. The letters he wrote to the churches in Corinth, Rome, Ephesus, Colossae, Philippi, Galatia, Thessalonica, and to leaders such as Timothy, Titus, and Philemon all trumpet his amazement, gratitude, and certainty that God's heart for sinners like you and me is to make us "good enough" for an eternal relationship with Him. He does it as we believe.

For Further Thought:

1) Have you ever done anything you were absolutely convinced was absolutely right for all the right reasons. . .and then discovered you were completely wrong? What was your reaction? Did you want to hide it? Manipulate circumstances or opinions to appear simply misunderstood or not as blatantly wrong as you were? What would it have taken for you to immediately take ownership of your error and begin to rectify it as Saul did?

2) If you are reading this book, you are probably considered to be a very good person. Do you see any areas in yourself others may not know, but where you might agree with Jesus that you are actually behaving as an enemy to Him? If so, what would it take for you to truly call Jesus "Lord" in these areas?

6

"I Am Not Ashamed of the Gospel"
(Romans 1:16)

———————

As Paul traveled, planting churches all around the Mediterranean rim, he had a deep connection with the people and a steady concern that they would know and live the true Gospel they had received. He knew his own system of trying to please God had never succeeded. His best efforts were never enough. It would be the same for them. He knew only the true Gospel would make them good enough for God. So, he wrote letters. A letter for a particular church was intensely valuable, so they consumed it, and then passed it among the other churches. In this way, all could benefit.

The apostle wrote to the Romans while he was in the Greek city of Corinth in AD 57, just three years after sixteen-year-old Nero had become

Emperor of Rome. At the time of the writing, Christians were doing reasonably well in Rome. We know Nero as a hater of the church, and one of the most heinous tyrants ever. However, Nero would not begin his infamous persecution of Christians until he made them scapegoats after the raging Roman fire in AD 64. It was unclear whether accident or arson caused the fire that decimated the city, but shortly after the fire, he began to build himself a huge palace in the center of Rome, called "the Golden House." This caused some people to surmise the fire had been deliberately set to enable his building project. In order to diffuse blame, Nero targeted the Christians, who had always been different. Their devotion to a man once crucified, said to be alive again, their loyalty to one another and sense of community, their references to "blood that was precious," and such deviations from what was normative for people of the day distinguished them. But despite their differences, Paul was writing then to a church that was in a period of peace and relative acceptance by the culture. Paul knew that the greatest thing to fear was misplaced faith, and he felt they needed a strong dose of basic truth.

Paul actually had not yet visited Rome. He did not establish the church there. The Roman church was likely the result of one or two Romans who were in Jerusalem on the Day of Pentecost (Acts 2:10) who returned to their home, changed by the Gospel and full of the Spirit's power. When the Emperor Claudius had expelled the Jews from Rome in AD 49, the Gentile Christians formed house churches for meeting. When Nero began his reign, he allowed the Jews to return to Rome, and the church at the time of Paul's writing was composed of both Jews and Gentiles. He clearly expressed his strong desire to travel there in the near future (Acts 19:21; Romans 1:10–12), and personalized his letter by greeting more than two dozen people by name. This provided personal credibility to the recipients, as most of them would view him as a stranger. This was typical Paul, making sure to connect in a way that would give the Gospel its best hearing. The church was undoubtedly large when Paul wrote. Saint Clement wrote in AD 96 that when Nero persecuted the Christians from 64–67, less than a decade after Paul wrote that, "a great multitude of the elect" were martyred.

Paul's location in the city of Corinth put him in the center of a cultural hotbed. A quick browse of Paul's letters written to the Corinthians will show that Paul was well aware of the diverse array of people and practices there and in the world in general—from gruff sailors and talkative tradesmen to wealthy idolaters and enslaved Christians. He addressed specific issues in this church that aren't addressed in any other letters, because the church was so affected by the culture. Corinth was well known for the most perverted kinds of sexual immorality and a wide buffet of idol worship. His pristine Jewish upbringing had long ago lost its ability to cocoon him from the world. As a Corinth resident, from his own windows and doorstep Paul was privy to a daily display of the sinfulness of humanity. He also witnessed in the Corinthian believers an ongoing remarkable demonstration of the power of God to miraculously and completely change lives. In 1 Corinthians 6, Paul makes a long list of what most commonly would make the "worst of the worst" list of sinners, saying those who are guilty of these deeds will not be part of the Kingdom of God. Then he declares, "But this is what many of you were until the power of God cleaned you and made you acceptable to a holy God!"

Prompted by these surroundings, and driven by love for all the churches, starting with the thriving Roman believers, Paul writes the clearest and most systematic presentation of the Gospel in all the scriptures. The study of what he wrote to the Romans has proven through the centuries to be life changing for multitudes of seekers. In 386, Augustine, the one we now know as Saint Augustine, sat weeping alone in a garden, considering his need of radical change in his chaotic life. He was wayward, lost by most anyone's description. A child ran through the neighborhood singing a childish tune, and a repeated line invited, "Take up and read." A scroll was lying near where he sat in the friend's garden, and he picked it up and began to read these words from Paul: "Not in rioting and drunkenness, not in chambering and wantonness, not in strife and envying. But put ye on the Lord Jesus Christ, and make not provision for the flesh, to fulfill the lusts thereof" (Romans 13:13–14 KJV). He repented and from that moment on, began to lead a new life.

Augustine some years later recorded his response to the words he read from Paul: "No further would I read, nor had I any need; instantly, at the end of this sentence, a clear light flooded my heart and all the darkness of doubt vanished away" (Confessions, viii. 29). A man whose life was distinguished by immorality and self-centered living became a man whose life so imitated Christ that he became a priest, a writer, and a Christian leader who is admired and shaping the world yet today.

Many years later, in November of 1515, Martin Luther was an Augustinian monk teaching at the University of Wittenberg. As he taught Paul's letter to the Romans to his students, he found himself struggling to reconcile what he was reading with what he had been taught about a relationship with God. He could not comprehend it. Luther described his spiritual and intellectual struggle this way: "I greatly longed to understand Paul's Epistle to the Romans, and nothing stood in the way but that one expression, 'the righteousness of God,' because I took it to mean that righteousness whereby God is righteous and deals righteously in punishing the unrighteous. . . . Night and day I pondered until. . .I grasped the truth that the righteousness of God is that righteousness whereby, through grace and sheer mercy, he justifies us by faith. Thereupon I felt myself to be reborn and to have gone through open doors into paradise. The whole of Scripture took on a new meaning, and whereas before 'the righteousness of God' had filled me with hate, now it became to me inexpressibly sweet in greater love. This passage of Paul became to me a gateway to heaven."

Luther's understanding that a person does not perform his or her way into acceptance by God changed his life and eternity. He recorded it as his moment of conversion. It not only lit a fire in his heart, this truth burned its way through the culture, creating the Protestant Reformation. Clearly, the changed Luther continues impacting lives even today.

More than 200 years later, a troubled young Anglican cleric frequently made distraught journal entries about his lack of confidence relating to God. John Wesley desperately wanted to be approved by God, so much so that he and several friends founded "the Holy Club" while students at Oxford University. At personal peril, Wesley also traveled as a missionary to the colonies, attempting to convert the Native Americans. During a pounding storm on the return journey, he was panicked and overwrought. In the midst of his anxiety, he was impressed by the completely different level of faith in a group of German Christians, believers who had learned what Luther discovered. On January 24, 1738, he wrote in his journal, "I went to America, to convert the Indians; but oh! Who shall save me?"

John Wesley went to a London church later that same year and heard Luther's comments on Romans read by the pastor. In his journal, Wesley wrote: "I went very unwillingly to a society in Aldersgate Street, where one was reading Luther's Preface to the Epistle to the Romans. . . . About a quarter before nine while he was describing the change which God works in the heart through faith in Christ, I felt my heart strangely warmed.

I felt I did trust in Christ, Christ alone, for my salvation; and an assurance was given me that he had taken my sins away, even mine; and saved me from the law of sin and death." He became a flaming firebrand, heading the eighteenth-century Evangelical Revival and impacting the entire world with his ministry yet today.

Karl Barth is known as one of the most influential theologians of the twentieth century. The book of Romans so captivated him that he wrote a commentary on it, and then his continued studies caused him to almost completely revise it. In his thoroughly rewritten second edition of 1922, Barth argued that the mercy and grace of God revealed in the cross of Jesus as the sole method of becoming right with God, challenges and overthrows any attempt to relate to God through human achievement or performance. He never got past it.

While not all theologians or biblical scholars have experienced the documented dramatic changes which the book of Romans produced in these men and many more, all are virtually unanimous concerning the monumental significance and eternal contribution of this letter Paul wrote. Countless ordinary people since Paul penned the letter so many years ago have believed his words and so discovered how the gap can be bridged between a hopelessly broken and sinful human, and a totally holy God. In fact, one of the best-known simple explanations developed for one person to share salvation with another is known as "the Roman Road." It is a simple yet powerful method of explaining the need of salvation using verses from Romans—how God provided salvation, how we can receive salvation, and what are the results of salvation. Paul reaches back to his spiritual and Jewish father, Abraham, to make sense of this radical thinking about relationship with God.

As the letter begins, Paul greets the Romans, and establishes his credentials as a spokesman for God and His church. As a Jew writing to both Jews and Gentiles, he says they are his equals: called by God just as he is to belong to Jesus, loved by God just as he is, and called to be His holy people, just as he is. He blesses them with grace and peace, and assures them of his desire to come see them in person. Paul says he is eager to come and preach the Gospel to them, since, "I am not ashamed of the gospel, because it is the power of God that brings salvation to everyone who believes: first to the Jew, then to the Gentile" (Romans 1:16 NIV).

That Gospel occupies his pen the rest of the letter, and contains the one and only way anyone can become good enough for God.

For Further Thought:

1) Augustine, Luther, Wesley, and Barth are not just historical names. If you are a Christ follower, look at your family tree. Jesus died on the cross, paid the debt for our sins, rose again, and left His followers the Gospel message with the command (known as the Great Commission) to take it to the whole world.

   A short while after Jesus ascended into heaven, Saul/Paul met Jesus on the road to Damascus, understood the message of salvation, and became a passionate messenger. A decade or so after that, Paul wrote the letter to the Romans, systematically detailing the liberating truth of the Gospel.

   Three hundred some years later, the words Paul had written jumped off the page into Augustine's heart and transformed him. His life, writing, and words were central in the ongoing growth of the church of Jesus Christ, known primarily as the catholic, or universal, church. In the Apostles' Creed, the statement, "I believe in the holy catholic church" is applicable even to believers who are not part of the current Catholic church, a branch of the Body of Christ. The word "catholic" simply meant anyone, anywhere who had put their faith in Christ—this made up the Church.

The leadership of the church got away from the basic truths of the Gospel over time, forgetting some essentials and adding to the simple faith. Martin Luther discovered that truth by studying the book of Romans and then protested in the 1500s, igniting the Protest-ant (Protestant Reformation), which also reawakened many remaining followers in the Roman Catholic Church to the true Gospel.

Without a continued focus on the core of the Gospel, however, it is a matter of time before deterioration occurs. In the 1700s all of Europe was in need of a great awakening.

John Wesley came alive to the words God had given Paul initially for the Romans, and his conversion led England to a great revival, sparing it from the bloody revolutions that ravaged France and the rest of Europe.

A few hundred more years down the road, Karl Barth studied Augustine, Luther, and Wesley—they all led him back to Paul and Romans. Barth's works have shaped the church today, and have been read by your pastor, or you, if you have been a theological student.

Today you are reading a book about the simple Gospel truth of how lost sinners can become good enough for God, a book based in the truth Jesus spoke to Paul. Amazing family line, right?

2) Make sure to not just read about Romans. Start today by reading the first chapter of Romans, and every day actually read the sections we will discuss in the rest of this book.

7

"There Is None Righteous, No, Not One" (Romans 3:10)

―――――――

Bruce Almighty is a 2003 comedy film about Bruce Nolan, a down-on-his-luck TV reporter who has a dream of being the news anchorman. Bruce is passed over for the promotion in favor of his coworker and rival. He rages during a live on-air interview, which leads to his suspension from the station. A series of misfortunes follows, and Bruce complains to God that God isn't doing His job correctly. To his astonishment, the Almighty appears and offers Bruce the chance to try being God for one week. Bruce tries his hand at it, and in a nanosecond he sees that the things that seemed simple from his one-sided, uninformed perspective aren't anything like he thought.

My mother knew that. Oftentimes in my

childhood I remember her saying, "Oh, I am so glad I am not God!" She meant that decisions involving real live people who will live forever somewhere are complex and challenging. It's good that God is the One in charge of determining destinies.

Just considering the situations of Abram/ Abraham, Aaron, and Dismas gives us a peek into how disparate our circumstances are. We might hope that God would grade on the curve, just averaging out the worst and the best, but how could a holy, just God do that? There has to be a standard, a true and equitable criterion, but as the psalmist said, "If you, LORD, kept a record of sins, Lord, who could stand?" (Psalm 130:3 NIV). What can be done for sinful man to make it possible for any of us, from the best of us to the worst of us, to have a relationship with, and a future with, a God of infinite perfection and holiness?

The apostle Paul wanted the people in the great city of Rome to understand exactly mankind's dilemma, and what God said about the possibility of sinful humanity being good enough. Paul wrote them and explained in the first sentences that God had called him to tell this good news. But a person has to know how bad the bad news is before he can appreciate and act on the good news. Paul unequivocally states the bad news. He takes a walk on the dark side, compellingly illustrating the hopeless situation of mankind. Paul holds nothing back, pulls no punches in his exposé of human depravity in the last half of Romans 1—it's ugly, bleak, scandalous, appalling. Like a prosecuting attorney, Paul adds piece after piece of incriminating evidence. We almost feel embarrassed as he describes pagan, godless humanity. The Roman Christians must have felt, at this point in their journey at least, as most of us feel as he describes the lowest levels of religious practices, sexual activities, and criminal acts. Depravity is on parade. Certainly, these people are not acceptable to God. These humans have practically lost their God-given humanity, and they have willingly consented to perversion and darkness. Chaos and disorder appear to be the current consequences of their choices.

But Paul continues. He describes more sinners, more people who are not good enough for God. The sinners he chronicles in chapter 2 are "good sinners," self-righteous, people who believe that their performance is so outstanding, they can afford to look down upon and pass judgment on others. He specifically points out Jews, who perform to please God, as Paul once did. They don't get it. They are missing the point. They believe that God's kindness to them is a reward for their goodness. The "good sinners" do not understand that their circumstances are only the result of God's patience and mercy. He is delaying judgment to give them also opportunity for repentance (2:5).

Paul knew he had to make that fact crystal clear, because Jews, like Aaron, the rich young ruler, believed they were special. Because they are children of Abraham, the people God called His own, they assumed they were exempt from judgment. Paul sets the facts straight. The Jews are just as guilty as the Gentiles. They are as far off the mark as the rest of the world. He describes their way of thinking, and then asks rapid-fire, rhetorical questions, and reminds them that the real work of God is seen internally in the heart.

"Now you, if you call yourself a Jew; if you rely on the law and boast in God; if you know his will and approve of what is superior because you are instructed by the law; if you are convinced that you are a guide for the blind, a light for those who are in the dark, an instructor of the foolish, a teacher of little children, because you have in the law the embodiment of knowledge and truth–you, then, who teach others, do you not teach yourself? You who preach against stealing, do you steal? You who say that people should not commit adultery, do you commit adultery? You who abhor idols, do you rob temples? . . .A person is a Jew who is one inwardly; and circumcision is circumcision of the heart, by the Spirit, not by the written code" (2:17–22, 29 NIV).

Frankly, Paul says, "Are we Jews better than the rest of the world? Not at all. We are all under the domination of sin" (3:9). To prove his point, he calls witnesses who stand tall in Jewish history.

- King David: The most revered king of Israel, they knew the scriptures recorded God's assessment of David as a "man after God's own heart" (1 Samuel 13:13–14).

- King Solomon: David's son was the richest, wisest, most powerful man in his time and put Israel on the map.
- Isaiah: One of the greatest prophets in Jewish history, his uncompromising convictions made him one of the most powerful examples in all of the Old Testament.

Paul was very familiar with the words these men had recorded, and he blended them together in a brief, indicting discourse on fallen and hopeless mankind.

"As it is written: 'There is no one righteous, not even one; there is no one who understands, no one who seeks God. All have turned away, they have together become worthless; there is no one who does good, not even one.' 'Their throats are open graves; their tongues practice deceit.' 'The poison of vipers is on their lips.' 'Their mouths are full of cursing and bitterness.' 'Their feet are swift to shed blood; ruin and misery mark their ways, and the way of peace they do not know.'

'There is no fear of God before their eyes'" (Paul is quoting Psalm 14:1–3, 53:1–3, Ecclesiastes 7:20, Psalm 5:9, Psalm 140:3, Psalm 10:7, Isaiah 59:7–8, Psalm 36:1).

The conclusion is damning.

No one is righteous, not even one. That's not Aaron, not your Grandma, not Billy Graham.

No one understands. Not Albert Einstein, not your class valedictorian, not your therapist.

No one on his own initiative seeks God. Not a single one of history's witnesses who exclaim, "I found God!"

No one does good. No, not one. Not even Mother Teresa.

Everyone practices deceit, and poison is on our lips. Even Honest Abe.

No one knows the way of peace. Not Jimmy Carter, Mahatma Gandhi, or Martin Luther King.

Now that's bleak.

You have to be righteous to be good enough for God, but no one is.

If any less than David, Solomon, and Isaiah had said it, no one would believe it. That's why Paul called the all-star list of witnesses.

We don't use the words "righteous" or "righteousness" frequently in our daily conversations. We will, however, describe someone as "self-righteous." The term refers to someone whose smug, personal opinion of himself is that he is morally superior to others, sanctimonious, looking at others condescendingly and critically. Righteousness actually is not being better than someone else, even most of the someone elses. Righteousness actually is the state of moral perfection required by God to have a saving relationship with Him and enter heaven.

Self-righteous people fall into the comparison trap in evaluating their righteousness. As long as they compare favorably with others, they believe they pass the test. Many of us are performers, and we look for the rules for behavior that make us acceptable, trying to keep the most important ones.

How do you believe a person can be good enough for God? What is the standard? On what are you pinning your hopes? Ask a sampling of people how they believe a person closes the gap between God's perfect righteousness in a holy heaven and mankind's sinfulness. Most everyone will say there is a connection between how well we perform and making the grade. The reasoning follows a reasonable pattern: "Good people go to heaven. When we behave well enough, it is only fair to get a reward, and when we behave badly, it is only fair to be punished."

Follow that up with, "And you. . .are you good enough?" There may be a little blushing and a few disclaimers issued, but essentially everyone you asked would conclude that, yes, they were fairly confident they are good enough. It is extremely rare to officiate at a funeral where anyone has anything but confidence that the deceased has made it to heaven, even if he or she never spoke of God and lived a dark life. Family members search for some redeeming action the person has done, a prayer they prayed at age five in vacation Bible school, or an excuse for vile behavior.

Press them further and ask what personally makes them good enough. "I don't lie, I don't steal, I give to the poor, and I keep the Ten Commandments." Here's the problem. No one becomes right with God by obeying the law. In fact, that wasn't even the reason God gave the law. God primarily gave the Ten Commandments to Moses to share with the people so they could live in community and get along. The first commandments were about their relationship with Him, telling them who He was (Exodus 20), and the rest were about how people were to treat each other to enable them to live cooperatively and healthily. But soon after receiving the commandments, the people messed up. Moses went back to Mt. Sinai, the place where he talked with God face to face and received direction, and in his absence for only a short time, the people were unable to keep just these ten rules (Exodus 32). When Moses came down from the mountain and saw them in the middle of their sin, carrying stone tablets on which the finger of God had engraved the commandments, he was so angry he threw and broke the tablets. His brother Aaron told him, "Don't be so shocked. You know the hearts of the people are set on evil" (Exodus 32:22).

That's typical. License Bureaus state it is not unusual for a person who has just passed their driver's test, knowing all the rules well enough to score high on the written section and drive correctly with an examiner in the car, to get a ticket for breaking a rule within the first week of driving.

The law is incapable of making us perform well enough to meet the standard. Paul clearly states to the Romans that human beings cannot achieve righteousness through their own efforts: "Therefore no one will be declared righteous in God's sight by the works of the law; rather, through the law we become conscious of our sin" (Romans 3:20 NIV). The law, or the Ten Commandments, shows us how far we fall short of God's standards.

It's like me driving down the road near my home. It is a beautiful straight stretch with few bumps. Even though I have driven this road multiplied thousands of times over the years, it is so easy to break the speed limit. I will be caught up in life, breezing along, when my eyes catch a glimpse of the law, a white and black speed limit sign posted on the side of the road. Instantly my foot reaches for the brake, working frantically to pull me back within acceptable limits before I am caught. I have been caught on this road. Less than a half mile from our house, a uniformed sheriff's deputy turned on his lights and sirens, and motioned me to the side of the road a few years ago. He was very pleasant, and agreed with me that my violation was not malicious, that I wasn't rebellious or arrogant, but firmly told me my attitude and intentions did not alter the fact the I had broken the law. The signpost was power-less to equip or force me to meet the standard; it simply served as a witness to how far I was off the mark.

What about the time-honored direction to "Let your conscience be your guide"? Will that work? Many people believe that the way to be good enough for God is to follow the inner GPS God has given you. Don't stray from that internal ticker and you will be fine. The problem is, that's not fair. Cultures differ within families and communities. What is permissible for one will be verboten for another. Whose standard prevails?

Even if we could agree on one standard to fit all, what grade would be acceptable? What would be the cutoff? What percentage of "getting it right" would it take?

Imagine this. The Bible says that our sins have separated us from God (Isaiah 59:2), and the gap is so large, He can't even hear us. Let's say that human beings have been challenged to swim the oceanic gap between the shores of the Outer Banks of the United States to the coastal town of Poole, England. Anyone who makes the trip successfully will receive a hero's welcome, and be guaranteed a relationship with God and an eternal heavenly home.

Masses of humanity gather on the shore, positively thinking, hoping, and praying. Some only watch and don't even try. They know it is hopeless; the Atlantic is far too big. They quickly lose interest and go back to town to entertain themselves in other ways. Babies, children, and the disabled try valiantly, but most of them drown within 6 feet of the shoreline. There is much anguish and anger—there should have been a different standard for them! I am a poor swimmer—I can barely stay afloat in our five-feet-deep pool. So though I give it my best, I and many like me go under, never to be seen again only about fifteen feet out. There are varying degrees of success, some of the best swimmers going a mile or more. Mark Spitz and Michael Phelps are there, both Olympic gold medal swimmers. They get so far out, their bodies are mere specks on the horizon. Michael Phelps is younger, the winner of eighteen gold medals, more than any other swimmer in Olympic history, twice the number earned by Spitz. He is the last to go under, finally disappearing beneath the dark waves. In the end, it doesn't matter how far out anyone can swim. The standard is too high. The ocean is too wide. No one can do it. Some do far better than others, but in the end, everyone fails. Everyone drowns. Human beings just don't have the capacity for the task.

That describes the human dilemma. The job of being good enough for God is impossible. We attempt it, with varying degrees of success, but even the best of us fall short. The gap between our sinfulness and His holiness is far too wide. Gospel singer Squire Parsons described the gulf separating him from Christ the Lord as "vast, the crossing I could never ford." God's perfect demands were so far that he cried out in song, "O God, I cannot come to where you are!" No one can. Eventually we all drown.

So what's the hope? Why would God even suggest or desire a relationship with sinful human beings if we are incapable of being good enough? If all of us fail, what's the point? If it is true, as Paul said, that, "all the world is guilty before God" (3:19), what was God thinking? Paul leads us right back to Abram.

For Further Thought:

1) Take time to read Romans 3:1–20. Do you think Paul is overstating it, or do these words ring true for you?

2) Take a newspaper with you, go to a quiet place, and browse through it for fifteen minutes. Circle any evidence that the world in which you live is aptly described in 3:10–18.

8

"This Righteousness Is Given Through Faith in Jesus Christ to All Who Believe"
(Romans 3:22)

———————

Paul's systematic presentation of the solution to the problem is as uplifting as his presentation of the problem was devastating. No one is righteous; not one will ever be good enough for God on his own merit. It is impossible that anyone will ever keep the law well enough to boast or brag that they have earned their standing with God. But God has made a way.

Paul called on the Jewish heroes to bear witness to the depravity of mankind. Now he calls on Abram, renamed Abraham, (Genesis 17:5, since God was making him the Father of many nations) for an explanation of what God has done. He asks, "What did Abraham, our physical forefather, discover about this? If Abraham did something to earn or deserve God's selection of him, he truly had something to brag about. But what does God's recorded story tell us? 'Abraham believed God, and it was credited to him for righteousness.'" Paul was quoting God's direct words recorded for all time in Genesis 15:6.

These words were so significant to Paul, explaining beyond a doubt the divine plan for making sinners good enough for God, that he wrote the same thing in his letter to the church at Galatia:

> *So again I ask, does God give you his Spirit and work miracles among you by the works of the law, or by your believing what you heard? So also Abraham "believed God, and it was credited to him as righteousness." Understand, then, that those who have faith are children of Abraham. Scripture foresaw that God would justify the Gentiles by faith, and announced the gospel in advance to*

Abraham: "All nations will be blessed through you." So those who rely on faith are blessed along with Abraham, the man of faith.

GALATIANS 3:5–9 NIV

As Paul passionately pens his letter, his go to illustration is always Abraham. Remember, he grew up as an elite Jewish boy, well-schooled, and Abraham was his hero. The realization that God had dealt with him in the very same manner as the man he and all his people revered, was intoxicating. God had provided for a clean and personal relationship with him just as he did for Abraham? Well, he just couldn't quit talking about it. He had to share the good—no, incredible—news. Several specifics in Chapter 4 capture his awe:

The time frame when Abraham's faith was credited as righteousness (4:10–12). His readers were fully informed that good Jews had to be circumcised, and that many Jews expected believing Gentiles to be circumcised, too. But Paul breathlessly asks, "When did God count Abraham's belief as good enough—before he was circumcised or after he was circumcised?"

He quickly answers his own question: Not after, but before! Abraham was circumcised because of his covenant relationship with God, not in order to have it. God approved of him just because of his faith. This makes him the father of all the faithful, whether they are circumcised or not. Eugene Peterson in *The Message* describes this "crediting" as "being set right by God and with God!" (4:12)

The reason for God's promises to Abraham (4:13–15). God sought out Abraham to have a relationship with Him and bless Him because He wanted to, not because Abraham impressed Him. He didn't get God's attention by living like a saint; God loved Abraham and chose him when he was a nobody. Abraham was able to step into what God wanted to give him because he simply believed God and acted on it.

The focus of Abraham's faith (4:16–22). Abraham was called "father" before he was a father. He had to believe it. And it was not natural or easy to believe. Every day he carried around his hundred-year-old body, with its accompanying aches and pains. He knew he wasn't the man he once was, and he knew he was past natural capacity to father a child. Every day, Sarah's wrinkled eighty-five-year-old face looked across the breakfast table at him. They had weathered decades of disappointment and infertility together. But one day he cast all doubts aside and plunged right into the promise of God. He quit focusing on what he was and was not, and fixed his focus squarely on what God said. He decided to believe with all his heart that God was great enough and good enough to come through on the promise. When his faith was completely in God, not in himself, his faith made him right with God.

The good news for Abraham's children (4:23–25). Again, *The Message* states the most wonderful news known to mankind in plain words any man or woman can understand:

But it's not just Abraham; it's also us! The same thing gets said about us when we embrace and believe the One who brought Jesus to life when the conditions were equally hopeless. The sacrificed Jesus made us fit for God, set us right with God.

The good news is the same for us that it was for Abraham, Saul/Paul, Aaron (the rich young ruler), and Dismas (the thief on the cross)—becoming right with God is simply too big a job for any one of us. If it depended on us to make things right with God through our own efforts, we are forever without hope. We are in way over our heads. No matter how hard we work, no matter how long we work, we will always come up short. But we are put right with God *by* God, through believing and acting on what He said. It is simply, totally a sheer gift, paid for by Christ. If you are a nobody with nothing impressive about you, or if what is memorable is your sins and mistakes, you are a prime candidate for God. He is right now pursuing you. If you are impressive in all the right ways, and your resume of righteousness would make you an instant Eagle Scout with a bullet, He is still pursuing you. No matter how high you rise on the popular stock market, you will be light-years short.

Paul's letters were not written in chapters and verses like we have them in our New Testaments. They were written simply as long letters, and many years later divided into the style with which we are familiar for ease in finding, reading, and memorizing. Think of that, and look now at Romans chapter 5. Paul has just laid out his case for how dirty rotten scoundrels, broken and hopeless sinners, can become right with God. He personally knows this is fact, because he has been made right with God by placing his full faith in Jesus Christ, embracing with his whole heart God's method for restoring us to relationship. Can you see his pen flying over the papyrus, caught up in the thrill of what that actually means? Martin Luther said, "In the whole Bible there is hardly another chapter which can equal this triumphant text." He wants all of his readers to know this is more than an interesting concept, or a legal transaction—this gift is real, and opens the most remarkable blessings imaginable.

We are friends with God (5:1). We once were His enemies, far from Him, even if we didn't know it. Some people go quite a long way without realizing they are in trouble, like a driver blithely singing along with the radio, completely oblivious to the pursuing highway patrolman flashing his lights behind him. But ignorance doesn't change the fact that eventually the truth will catch up with us. The relationship He created us to have with Him was irreparably broken on our end. But now we have peace with God, friendship with God, relationship with God—and it is all because of our faith in Jesus Christ!

We receive God's grace (5:2). Sometimes it is said that grace is

God's
Riches
At
Christ's
Expense

That's not a bad way to describe it. We think of showing grace as showing favor and kindness to someone. Paul says we stand in grace, surrounded by the kindness and goodness of God. Grace is exactly what we need when we need it even when we don't know to ask for it. Grace is given before we ask. That's what makes it grace.

Paul says when we are made right with God, we "gain access" to God's grace. The door is thrown open for us. I remember seeing pictures of President John F. Kennedy's then tiny son called John-John playing in the space underneath his Daddy's large desk in the Oval Office. He played in his Daddy's presence, while important men of state waited for special permission for a few moments with the most powerful man in the world. John-John enjoyed freely what he could never have earned. He had access through grace. We are God's favored children, and we have a constant open door to His grace.

We have hope in God's glory (5:2). Typically people use the word "hope" when they mean, "I wish something would happen." But for Paul, hope always means "happy certainty" (J. B. Phillips). That means we can live with confidence and joy, because we have believed that whatever God says, He will do. To be able to live every day with happy confidence is priceless.

We have purpose in our problems (5:3–5). Our faith in Jesus Christ has set us right with God. We are at peace with Him. We still live in a broken and troubled world that often lacks peace and provides problems and pains. But we are different now! Our sufferings can't defeat us. We have "happy certainty" even in the middle of them, because we know how God works. When we suffer we learn to persevere; perseverance develops character in us; character leads to hope. And God's kind of hope never disappoints or buries us in shame, because we have constant access to God's replenishing love through His personal gift of the Holy Spirit. Paul knew this better than anyone. His life was full of problems and pain. But he was never under his circumstances. Why? Because God's love filled him up with purpose and confidence. He says God's love is poured out in our hearts. Not trickled or dripped over our hearts, but poured and running over.

We are loved beyond reason (5:6–11). Love is an overused word. We love french fries, the schnauzer puppy (even if he destroys a good shoe), music, the color blue, coffee, and even slightly obnoxious television series. We also love our spouse and Jesus. Seems a bit ridiculous, doesn't it? But at least when we get to people, we try to be a bit more discriminating and wise, saving our love for those who are worth it and return the love. It's only reasonable. Anyone could love a good person. Paul says it is rare, but love might be occasionally so deep for a truly good person that another would consider dying for them. Possibly. In contrast, the love we receive from God is utterly unreasonable. Jesus died for us. . .while we were still sinners. While we were His enemies. When there was nothing to love about us. What a demonstration of unreasonable, inexplicable love! If He loved us that much when we were His enemies, we have nothing to fear now that we are reconciled to Him.

Now Paul runs back for one more history lesson. I'll bet you can identify. Have you ever wanted to look up your great-great-great grandparents Adam and Eve, and just punch them for messing with that fruit? Paul agrees that our problems all go back to the Garden of Eden and their sin. He puts the weight of the responsibility on the first man, and reminds us that sin and death all came into the world as a result of the choice of that one man

Adam. Since that time, no person except Jesus has ever been born that is exempt from sin and death. It is staggering to think how completely sin and death have dominated humanity. Every single baby is born a sinner, and every single baby will die. The death rate is 100 percent. The only question is when. Sin separated Adam from God, and the entire landscape of history is bleak testimony to the destruction.

But Paul points past Adam to another man—Jesus Christ. He said just as one man brought death and separation from God into the world, one man brought everlasting life and reconciliation with God into the world. One man got us into a mess, and another man, the Messiah, got us out of the situation we could never fix. Only He could do it. We make a breath-taking recovery from our broken life when we simply trust God to do through Jesus what He said He would do.

Paul says something that is still hard for us to understand. He said that making laws against sin only makes more sinners (5:20). It's true. In our political campaigns, the phrase "You can't legislate morality" is tossed back and forth. We can make laws that hopefully will be a deterrent to evil behavior. But, just look at our prisons. They are overpopulated, full to the brim with people who were not made good by the laws. Even when they were fully aware of the probable punishment, they still stole, raped, and killed. You can make laws that punish people who do bad things, but you can't make bad people be good people by enacting laws.

Paul, an expert on this topic, had the proof of the Mosaic Laws, which the Jews included, were incapable of following. He said it is the very reason that Jesus Christ is necessary for our salvation. To argue for anything else is to deny the Christian faith. No law, and no amount of trying to be good will cut it. It is only by accepting the freely given gift of grace, by faith, that we are made good enough in God's eyes. "Consider Abraham," Paul says. "Our father Abraham knew it first."

And now, where sin abounded, God's grace superabounds. Where sin grew wild and free, God's grace is now wild and free. Does that mean don't worry about sinning because it's no big deal?

Not at all. That's Paul's next topic. How do people who have been made good enough for God live?

For Further Thought:

1) What wonderful good news that we are not expected to behave ourselves into relationship with God! Write or say a simple "thank you" prayer to God, for loving you just as you are.

2) Which of the benefits of this new relationship with God Paul lists in Chapter 5 are most exhilarating to you? Why?

9

"Alive to God in Christ Jesus"
(Romans 6:44)

———————

The question gets asked in dozens of ways, but the core of the issue is the same. Since God's heart for me is so strong, since He has made me good enough simply by my choice to believe and embrace His method for my salvation, what now? If God loves sinners, then why worry about sin? Since God understands our weaknesses and gives grace to sinners, since His forgiveness aggressively came looking for me, is it really that big a deal if I keep sinning? Paul asks, "Should we just keep on sinning so He can keep on forgiving?"

Is grace dangerous? Does grace invite me to abuse my relationship with God? Paul asks it this way, "Should we just keep on sinning so He can keep on forgiving?"

Paul practically interrupts his own question. "I should think not!" "Heaven forbid!" "By no means!" (Romans 6:1–2). No ambivalence here. Then Paul establishes an important principle. He reminds us that when we are set right with God by God, when we have believed on Jesus for our salvation, our relationship with sin is permanently changed. He likens it to death. We have died to sin. If we have died to sin, then we should not live any longer in habitual sin. It simply isn't fitting or reasonable to live any longer in something to which you have died.

Paul rejoices in the fact that God has done for sinners what we cannot do for ourselves. We didn't stop sinning in an effort to be loved and accepted by God. God Himself took all the initiative on opening the door to relationship. Now, as people who have been loved and accepted while we were still enemies, we are to respond like loved and forgiven people. He describes what that means:

> *Count yourselves dead to sin but alive*
> *to God in Christ Jesus. Therefore do not*
> *let sin reign in your mortal body so that*

*you obey its evil desires. Do not offer any
part of yourself to sin as an instrument of
wickedness, but rather offer yourselves to
God as those who have been brought from
death to life; and offer every part of yourself
to him as an instrument of righteousness.
For sin shall no longer be your master,
because you are not under the law, but
under grace.*

ROMANS 6:11–14 NIV

Practically speaking, that means that forgiven people in relationship with God have a new relationship with sin. If Paul was explaining it to you and me in a letter written today, he might say something like this:

*From now on, think of it this way:
Sin speaks a dead language that means
nothing to you; God speaks your mother
tongue, and you hang on every word. You
are dead to sin and alive to God. That's
what Jesus did. That means you must not
give sin a vote in the way you conduct your*

lives. Don't give it the time of day. Don't even run little errands that are connected with that old way of life. Throw yourselves wholeheartedly and full-time—remember, you've been raised from the dead!—into God's way of doing things. Sin can't tell you how to live. After all, you're not living under that old tyranny any longer. You're living in the freedom of God. 🏹

ROMANS 6:11–14 MSG

Over and over again Paul uses the images of freedom and slavery to describe how we are to now live. We are slaves to whatever and whoever we serve. These concepts were very real to all the Romans. Paul said, "Slavery to God is actually a life of freedom! You can walk in that freedom from sin as much as you choose."

A person can be officially, legally set free, yet still be imprisoned. *The Shawshank Redemption* cinematically portrays men who experienced the reality of being free without having freedom. Brooks, an elderly inmate, is paroled. He goes to a halfway house but finds it impossible to adjust to life outside the prison. He eventually commits suicide. When his friends suggest that he was crazy for doing so, another inmate named Red tells them that Brooks had obviously become "institutionalized," essentially conditioned to be a prisoner for the rest of his life, unable to adapt to the outside world. Red remarks, "At first you hate these walls, then you get used to 'em." Years later when Red himself is paroled, he finds he can't even go to the restroom without asking permission of someone as he used to ask the guard.

Spiritually, persons who have been slaves of sin often still think and act just like those prisoners. The habits of freedom aren't ingrained in their life yet. They don't realize they can choose. Paul says the daily choice of a person who is in right relationship with God must be the choice to give their appetites to God in service to Him. This is the path to increasing freedom.

In the fourteenth century two brothers battled for ruling rights over a dukedom in the country now known as Belgium. Edward, the younger brother, eventually defeated his older brother Raynald, and took over all his lands, becoming

Duke of everything. Raynald was nicknamed Crassus, a Latin word meaning "fat," because he was shockingly obese. When Edward conquered his brother, he chose to let him live instead of following the custom of killing defeated enemies. He devised an unconventional imprisonment for him. He had a room in the castle built to house Raynald. The windows were not barred, the door was not locked. Edward told Raynald he could walk out to freedom any time he chose to, and Edward would restore his lands and title. All he had to do was walk out.

But there was the problem. The door was a normal size, and Raynald far exceeded the limits of normal. The obstacle was Raynald himself. All Raynald needed to do was diet down to a smaller size and walk free. But to do so, he had to deny himself. His brother would send him an assortment of delectable food every day, as well as healthy, lower calorie food. Raynald's desire to be free never won out over his desire to satisfy his appetite.

That is the picture of life for many Christians. God has done for us through Jesus what we could never do for ourselves. Jesus has set us free, and we can walk in that freedom from sin whenever we choose. But since we keep giving in to our appetites, we keep choosing to serve sin, we live lives of defeat, discouragement and imprisonment. We say, "I prayed and I prayed. It doesn't work for me." But Paul says, "Sin is no longer your master." Charles Spurgeon, a nineteenth century preacher and revivalist, said these words are at the same time a test, a promise, and an encouragement. How so?

- A test of our claim to be Christians: Does sin have control over us much the same as it did before we came to Christ? If so, that's an issue.
- A promise of victory: It doesn't say we will never do battle with sin, that we will never be tempted. It promises that we do not have to let sin master us any longer. We have the power to choose in the strength of Christ.
- An encouragement for hope and strength in the battle: God has set me free in Jesus. I can get up and go again. Sin is not my master.

I had a counseling appointment with a young married woman. She deeply loves her wonderful husband, meant every word of her vows, and he is equally committed to her. She ran into an old boyfriend at the mall one day, and they had a cordial five-minute conversation, filling each other in on family news and current events. A few days later he friended her on Facebook and began sending her messages, asking her to meet for a casual lunch in a very public place. She politely declined. He mildly chastised her for her unwillingness to be friends with him. "I just want to be friends. In public. Talking just like we did in the mall. What's wrong with that?" She asked several friends about it, and they didn't see the harm in "just a lunch" either.

That's what landed my young friend in my office chair. She asked, "Is it prudish of me to not be comfortable spending time with a man I once loved, now that I am married to someone else?" I felt like Paul. "Heavens, no!" "God forbid!" "Certainly not!"

In light of our new relationship with God, it is utterly incompatible for a new creation in Jesus

Christ to be comfortable in habitual sin. His or her new commitment makes the old commitments and behavior distasteful. A state of sin can only be temporary for a Christian. Like the chance meeting in the mall, we can bump into sin, but our deepest desire is to take care not to arrange for it, to not make room for it. It's just not comfortable for us any longer. Our hearts are sad and broken when we sin, and we want to change it as soon as possible. Spurgeon further said, "Grace that does not change my life will not save my soul."

Jesus Himself said the difference between being right with God and being in sin is the same as the difference between life and death. That's a major difference. If you go to a funeral home, there's no problem for even a child to figure out who isdead and who is alive. John, another follower changed by Jesus, stated it this way: Whoever abides in Him does not (habitually) sin. Whoever (habitually) sins has neither seen Him nor known Him. . . Whoever has been born of God does not (habitually) sin, for his seed remains in him; and he cannot (habitually) sin, because he has been born of God (1 John 3:6, 9 NIV). All the changes may not come at the same time, and they may not come to each area of life at the same time. But the appetite for sin will keep decreasing as we keep choosing to live like people made alive in Christ; new characteristics and habits will come into our lives, and they will increase over time.

Let's think about Sally. She feels lost and broken much of the time. Though she works hard at the beautiful, together appearance she musters up each morning for her downtown job, she struggles with anger that goes back many years. Her husband and her daughter are treated to daily doses of rage, spiced with sarcasm and criticism. No one knows it, but she secretly wonders if she has become addicted to her pain pills from a fall a couple of years ago. She needs them to get through the day. Oh, yes. Did I mention she is a terrible cook? Dinner is usually whatever each one can find, eaten at the counter. Cereal boxes line the pantry.

Her coworker Deena has invited her to church several times, and she is intrigued by what she sees in Deena. She goes to Deena's church with her, feels a quick connection there, and can hardly wait for the next Sunday to come. On the second Sunday, she hears the Gospel message, that her emptiness and sin was paid for by Jesus Christ. All she has to do is believe and accept what He has done as payment for her sins. It seems too easy, but in a giant leap of faith, she believes, and is set right with God by God. Sally goes home elated and relieved, anxious for a new start. She even tells her husband and family what she has done, that everything is new, and that things are going to be different around here.

Then comes Monday morning. Getting off to a late start and the Monday morning traffic rush don't help her much, but the sheen hasn't rubbed off her experience yet. By afternoon, she is tired and anxious because new projects have come up at work without notice, and she really wants a pill. Make that, she needs a pill. She told herself yesterday she was done with them, but just one more. She runs through the pizza drive through on the way home, thinking she'll surprise Sonny and her daughter with dinner together. But when she walks through the door, no one is interested. They have already eaten an assortment of favorites already at home, and a trail of dirty dishes lead from the TV all the way to an already covered counter. Nothing is going as she hoped, and before the evening gets too far along, she has reverted to a sarcastic rant, leaving her daughter in tears and her husband withdrawn into video world. Just like a normal day?

Actually, no. Tonight is different. When her emotion is spent and Sally is alone, getting ready for bed, she feels very different. She cannot feel good about how she handled today. She has all the same reasons for reacting as she has every other day, but tonight the reasons aren't good enough. She slips into her daughter's room, loves on her, and asks forgiveness for the harsh words and attitudes. She says, "Darling girl, you are more than I could ask for. I love you so much. Jesus is going to help me be a better Mommy to you."

Sally pries her husband's attention away from the computer by putting her arms around his neck and then says, "I am so sorry. How could I expect you to read my mind? You couldn't have imagined I would bring pizza. Please forgive me. I love you."

Fast-forward three years. Three years of giving her appetites to Jesus, learning to live in the freedom his grace offers, refusing to be comfortable with old ways of life that Jesus gave her the power to make obsolete. Things surely are different in the orbit around Sally's life. At work she is valued as one who brings cooperation and optimism to difficult situations. The pills are long gone. She and her husband have a growing relationship of mutual respect, growing exponentially since he was set right with God, too. They have learned to communicate much better and share household responsibilities, each trying to serve the other. As her daughter is growing into a young teen, she and her mother still have disagreements over clothes and friends and concerts, but they really have fun, too. They love each other, and live up to their promises to never go to bed mad at one another. And the cooking thing? She still is no Paula Deen. But it has become important to Sonny and Sally that the family have dinner several nights a week together to they can talk and build memories. Between Pizza Hut, Chinese carryout, and her mom's old favorites, she can manage that. Life is good. Life is attractive. They have friends they have brought to Jesus and new life now, too.

See how that works? Jesus died for us, to make us acceptable to God, when we were totally unworthy. Totally unable to fix things for ourselves. We could never be good enough for God on our own. So God saved us, just by us believing and embracing what He had done through Jesus. But, because God has set us right with Him doesn't mean everything is right in every way in my life. If I am an addict, a bad cook, an angry rageaholic—you name it, from mild flaws or inabilities to major addictions—when God forgives me and sets me right with Him on Sunday, I am still going to be that on Monday. But now I have a choice. God has set me free from having to be a slave to that. I am justified. In His eyes, I am just-as-if-I-had never-sinned. Now He wants to work with His Spirit and my choices to sanctify me, to make me holy as His child. I can grow and change in every way that is harmful to the life God wants for me. Most changes won't happen overnight, although sometimes God chooses to do miraculous deliverances in an instant. Ordinarily, He works through my choices in my daily life to help me bear the family resemblance more and more.

That's what Paul talks about in the rest of his letter—establishing the habits that go with my new standing in the grace of Jesus Christ. It is the topic of most of his letters. He gives practical advice on relational issues, winning over habits, battling discouragement. He shares how we can be more than victorious in any and every situation we face, how we can discover and use the giftedness God has personally invested in us to live lives of significance. Paul shows us how the power of God in a person who is set right with God by God can now live in a way that gives the ultimate personal satisfaction, and gives honor to the One who paid such a price for us, a price we could never pay.

Some of Paul's most familiar words summarize the grateful life of one who has been made good enough for God:

Therefore, I urge you, brothers and sisters, in view of God's mercy [because of his amazing initiative and grace in your life] *to offer your bodies as a living sacrifice,*

holy and pleasing to God—this is your true
and proper worship. Do not conform to the
pattern of this world, but be transformed
by the renewing of your mind [work with
God, and refuse to be comfortable in
your old, sinful ways of life from which
Jesus died to set you free]. *Then you will*
be able to test and approve what God's
will is—his good, pleasing and perfect will
[you will find yourself fitting into every
wonderful thing God wants to provide
for his dearly loved child].

ROMANS 12:1–2 NIV

Abraham and Paul both discovered it. They
point the way for us. Now it is up to us to cooperate
with God's heart for people like us.

For Further Thought:

Read Romans 6–15 over the next two to three weeks. List all the characteristics, descriptions, and actions Paul says are appropriate for gratefully living free from the mastery of sin, and as a grateful grace recipient. Identify where you have been set free and where you still need to deny your appetites, and get out of the prison of your habits and choices. Make this part of your prayer list over the next few months, and then save it. Put it on your calendar to go back and read your list in six months, and see how you have changed.

Good Enough for God: The Romans Road

Maybe you have read this book and are still not entirely certain how you can ever be good enough for a holy God. Paul's letter to the Romans contains some very specific directions that have been called "the Romans Road," because they have been used to help many people understand how to be set right with God. If that is your desire, do what these verses say, and let God do for you what He wants to do and you need Him to do today.

- Romans 3:23 "For all have sinned, and come short of the glory of God" (KJV). We have all sinned. We have all done things that are displeasing to God. There is no one who is innocent. Agree with God that you can never close the gap between His standards and where you are.

- Romans 6:23 "For the wages of sin is death; but the gift of God is eternal life through Jesus Christ our Lord" (KJV). The consequences we have earned for our sins is death. Not just the physical death that came into the world through sin, but eternal death, separation from God, the source of life.

- Romans 5:8 "But God demonstrates His own love toward us, in that while we were yet sinners, Christ died for us" (NASB). Jesus Christ died for us! Jesus' death paid for the price of our sins. Jesus' resurrection is the ultimate and forever proof that God accepted Jesus' death as payment in full for our sins.

- Romans 10:9 "That if you confess with your mouth Jesus as Lord, and believe in your heart that God raised Him from the dead, you will be saved" (NASB). Because of Jesus' death on our behalf, all we have to do is believe in Him, trusting His death as the payment for our sins—and we will be saved.

- Romans 10:13 says it again, "For, 'Everyone who calls on the name of the Lord will be saved'" (NIV). This, trusting in the sacrifice of the Lord Jesus, is God's one and only method for sinners to become good enough for a holy God.

- Romans 5:1 "Therefore, since we have been justified through faith, we have peace with God through our Lord Jesus Christ" (NIV). Through Jesus Christ we can have a relationship of peace with God.

- Romans 8:1 "Therefore, there is now no condemnation for those who are in Christ Jesus" (NIV). Because of Jesus' death on our behalf, we are no longer condemned for our sins.

- Romans 8:38–39, "For I am convinced that neither death nor life, neither angels nor demons, neither the present nor the future, nor any powers, neither height nor depth, nor anything else in all creation, will be able to separate us from the love of God that is in Christ Jesus our Lord" (NIV). Nothing can separate us from God's love. That is the incredible message of the Gospel.

Here is a simple prayer. The words will not save you, but they are a way to declare to God that you are relying on Jesus Christ for your salvation.

"God, I know that I have sinned against You. I know I can never do anything to change the record by myself. I believe that Jesus Christ took the punishment that I deserve so that through faith in Him I can be forgiven and be made right with You. With Your help, I place my trust in Jesus for salvation. Thank You for Your gift of grace and forgiveness. Help me now to live free in You. Amen."

Scripture Index

Also from Barbour Publishing
By Dwight Mason,
Cowritten by Brenda Mason Young

Experience firsthand how Only God can use you—and the local church—to transform people, communities, the world. . . in an extraordinary way! You'll come away with a renewed sense of purpose, as you read Dwight Mason's powerful, life-altering message of hope. Get ready to let God work in and through you to change your world!

ISBN 978-1-61626-880-0 /
Paperback / 256 pages

Available wherever Christian books are sold.